Learn the Quran in

30

days of Ramadan

By
Quran & Islam

Acknowledgments

Reading the Quran in Arabic is great, but understanding its message is even greater. Dive deeper into the meaning and let the Quran guide your heart and mind.

Welcome to 'Learn the Quran in 30 Days of Ramadan'. This book takes you through 30 captivating stories from the Quran, bringing them to life in a way that makes them relatable and easy to understand.

This book is your guide to understanding the power of faith and the Quran. Here you will find heart-touching stories from the Quran that will help you deepen your faith and knowledge of the Quran. These stories will give you insight into the lives of the prophets and other figures mentioned in the Quran, and will inspire you to live a life guided by faith and understanding. Each story will also provide practical advice and lessons that you can apply to your own life. So come along on this journey of learning and growth, and let the Quran show you the way.

Each day, readers will delve into a new ayat, discovering its meaning, context, and significance through engaging stories and reflections. With this book, readers can enhance their Ramadan experience by connecting with the Quran on a deeper level and gaining a greater appreciation for its timeless teachings.

Contents

Story Number 1 1

"Habeel and Qabeel" The First Crime on Earth

Story Number 2: 4

Harut and Maarut, The Two Angels

Story Number 3:...7

The Heifer

Story Number 4: 9

Dwellers of the Town

Story Number 5 12

The Story of Uzair A.S.

Story number 6: 16

The Story of the Sabbath

Story Number 7: 18

Maryam A.S. : The Single Mother

Story Number 8: 22

Musa meets Khidr

Story Number 9:...26

The Pleading Woman

Story Number 10: 29

Qarun

Story Number 10: 33

The Queen of Sheba

Story Number 11: 37

The People of Saba

Story Number 12: 40

People of the Cave

Story Number 13: 46

The Believer and the Disbeliever

Story Number 14: 50

People of the Garden

Story Number 15: 54

The Verse of Feeding

Story Number 16: 56

Luqman the Wise Man

Story number 17: 60

The Pit of Fire

Story Number 18: 64

Barsisa the Worshipper

Story Number 19: 66

Repentance

Story Number 20: 68

Owners of the Elephant

Story Number 21: 73

Dhul Qarnayn

Story Number 22 77

    Ghazwa e Badr

Story Number 23: 79

    Asiya, the Foster Mother of Musa

Story Number 24: 84

    The Morning Sunlight

Stories 25: 87

    Hazrat Yusuf A.S.

Story Number 26: 97

    When the Earth is Shaken

Story Number 27: 100

    When Ibrahim built the House of Allah with His Son

Story Number 28: 106

    Allah raised Isa a.s to the Heavens

Story Number 29: 109

    Quran condemns Abu-Lahab

Story Number 30: 111

    When Ibrahim was in Fire

Conclusion 115

Story Number 1

"Habeel and Qabeel" The First Crime on Earth

Surat al-Maidah 27-31

وَٱتْلُ عَلَيْهِمْ نَبَأَ ٱبْنَىْ ءَادَمَ بِٱلْحَقِّ إِذْ قَرَّبَا قُرْبَانًا فَتُقُبِّلَ مِنْ أَحَدِهِمَا وَلَمْ يُتَقَبَّلْ مِنَ ﴿۞﴾ ٱلْءَاخَرِ قَالَ لَأَقْتُلَنَّكَ ۖ قَالَ إِنَّمَا يَتَقَبَّلُ ٱللَّهُ مِنَ ٱلْمُتَّقِينَ ٢٧

Relate to them in truth ˹O Prophet˺ the story of Adam's two sons—how each offered a sacrifice: Abel's offering was accepted while Qabeel's was not. So Qabeel threatened, "I will kill you!" His brother replied, "Allah only accepts ˹the offering˺ of the sincerely devout.

لَئِنۢ بَسَطتَ إِلَىَّ يَدَكَ لِتَقْتُلَنِى مَآ أَنَا۠ بِبَاسِطٍ يَدِىَ إِلَيْكَ لِأَقْتُلَكَ ۖ إِنِّىٓ أَخَافُ ٱللَّهَ رَبَّ ٱلْعَٰلَمِينَ ٢٨

If you raise your hand to kill me, I will not raise mine to kill you, because I fear Allah—the Lord of all worlds.

إِنِّىٓ أُرِيدُ أَن تَبُوٓأَ بِإِثْمِى وَإِثْمِكَ فَتَكُونَ مِنْ أَصْحَٰبِ ٱلنَّارِ ۚ وَذَٰلِكَ جَزَٰٓؤُا۟ ٱلظَّٰلِمِينَ ٢٩

I want to let you bear your sin against me along with your other sins, then you will be one of those destined to the Fire. And that is the reward of the wrongdoers."

فَطَوَّعَتْ لَهُ نَفْسُهُ قَتْلَ أَخِيهِ فَقَتَلَهُ فَأَصْبَحَ مِنَ ٱلْخَٰسِرِينَ ٣٠

Yet Qabeel convinced himself to kill his brother, so he killed him—becoming a loser.

1

فَبَعَثَ ٱللَّهُ غُرَابًا يَبْحَثُ فِى ٱلْأَرْضِ لِيُرِيَهُۥ كَيْفَ يُوَٰرِى سَوْءَةَ أَخِيهِ ۚ قَالَ يَـٰوَيْلَتَىٰٓ أَعَجَزْتُ أَنْ أَكُونَ مِثْلَ هَـٰذَا ٱلْغُرَابِ فَأُوَٰرِىَ سَوْءَةَ أَخِى ۖ فَأَصْبَحَ مِنَ ٱلنَّـٰدِمِينَ ٣١

Then Allah sent a crow digging ˹a grave˺ in the ground ˹for a dead crow˺, in order to show him how to bury the corpse of his brother. He cried, "Alas! Have I ˹even˺ failed to be like this crow and bury the corpse of my brother?" So he became regretful.

(no background) Adam A.S. used to get the male brought by one birth married to the female brought by the other. Hence, it was supposed that Abel would get married to Qabeel's sister who was better and more beautiful than anyone else. At the same time, Qabeel wanted to keep her for himself.

Adam A.S. ordered both Abeel and Qabeel to offer a sacrifice to Allah Almighty.

Meanwhile, Adam set forth towards Mecca to perform a Pilgrimage. Just before leaving, Adam entrusted the affairs of his children to Qabeel. After Adam went away, Abeel and Qabeel offered their sacrifices to Allah.

Abeel, a shepherd, offered a healthy ram as his best sacrifice. Whereas Qabil, a farmer, was not willing to give his best and offered some poor crops from his land.

Later, a fire came down from heaven and consumed the sacrifice offered by Abeel and left untouched that of Qabeel. Qabeel's sacrifice was not accepted.

Qabeel became livid with rage and said to his brother: I will kill you so as not to marry my sister, Abeel said:

Verily, Allah accepts only from those who are Al-Muttaqun (the pious).

'Abdullah Ibn `Amr (May Allah be pleased with both of them) said: *By Allah! Abeel, who was murdered, was stronger (than the murderer, Qabeel), but he refused to stretch his hand against his brother to kill him due to his piety and God-fearing.*

After Abeel's sacrifice was accepted, Qabeel said to his father, Adam: "It was accepted only from him because you invoked Allah for his sake."

Qabeel got angry and hit his brother with an iron rod at night, when he was sleeping, and Abeel fell dead at once.

After killing Habeel, Qabeel did not know what to do with his body. He carried him on his waist and came out looking for a way to dispose of his body. On the way, he saw two crows aggressively attacking each other which ultimately led to one crow killing the other. Then the crow that had killed the other crow started digging the earth and buried the crow that he had killed. This was the way Qabeel was taught how to bury his brother. Although Qabeel was sad about the heinous crime he had committed, he did not seek God's forgiveness. This made him a sinner and his name went down in history as the first killer on this earth.

Story Number 2:

Harut and Maarut, The Two Angels

Surah al-Baqarah 102

وَاتَّبَعُوْا مَا تَتْلُوا الشَّيْطِيْنُ عَلٰى مُلْكِ سُلَيْمٰنَ وَمَا كَفَرَ

سُلَيْمٰنُ وَلٰكِنَّ الشَّيٰطِيْنَ كَفَرُوْا يُعَلِّمُوْنَ النَّاسَ السِّحْرَ وَمَآ أُنْزِلَ عَلَى الْمَلَكَيْنِ بِبَابِلَ هَارُوْتَ وَمَارُوْتَ وَمَا يُعَلِّمٰنِ مِنْ اَحَدٍ حَتّٰى يَقُوْلَآ اِنَّمَا نَحْنُ فِتْنَةٌ فَلَا تَكْفُرْ فَيَتَعَلَّمُوْنَ مِنْهُمَا مَا يُفَرِّقُوْنَ بِهٖ بَيْنَ الْمَرْءِ وَ زَوْجِهٖ وَمَا هُمْ بِضَارِّيْنَ بِهٖ مِنْ اَحَدٍ اِلَّا بِاِذْنِ اللّٰهِ وَيَتَعَلَّمُوْنَ مَا يَضُرُّهُمْ وَلَا يَنْفَعُهُمْ وَلَقَدْ عَلِمُوْا لَمَنِ اشْتَرٰىهُ مَا لَهٗ فِى الْاٰخِرَةِ مِنْ خَلَاقٍ وَلَبِئْسَ مَا شَرَوْا بِهٖ اَنْفُسَهُمْ لَوْ كَانُوْا يَعْلَمُوْنَ ﴿٢:١٠٢﴾

"And they followed what the Shaitans chanted of sorcery in the reign of Sulayman, and Sulayman was not an unbeliever, but the Shaitans disbelieved, they taught men sorcery and that was sent down to the two angels at Babel, Harut and Marut, yet these two taught no man until they had said, "Surely we are only a trial, therefore do not be a disbeliever." Even then men learned from these two, magic by which they might cause a separation between a man and his wife; and they cannot hurt with it any one except with Allah's permission, and they learned what harmed them and did not profit them, and certainly they know that he who bought it should have no share of good in the hereafter and evil was the price for which they sold their souls, had they but known this". (2:102)

In these verses, Allah (SWT) refuted the false claims raised by the Children of Israel who said that Jibrael and Mikaeel brought magic down to the two Angels Harut and Marut. They also falsely stated that Prophet Suleiman (AS) was nothing but a sorcerer or idolater who was conveyed by the wind.

The demons used to ascend towards Paradise to decipher the discussions between the angels in regards to what will happen on Earth pertaining to matters that were veiled by Allah (SWT).

They would disseminate the news to the forecasters of the future and these forecasters and soothsayers would then pass on the news to the general population, who took the information to be relevant, valid and authentic. These tactics were used by the devils to lure in the soothsayers, and they soon began to manipulate the dialogues in an attempt to mislead the masses.

The general population recorded these so called 'truths' in a few books and before long, the Children of Israel started to believe that the Jinns know matters of the Unseen and lost faith in the fact that only Allah (SWT) holds the supreme power of what lies in the unseen.

Fortunately, when Prophet Suleiman (AS) was sent as a Prophet, he summoned all these books and buried them under his authority. Any devil that desired access to the vault was thus burnt.

He was so strict about this that Prophet Suleiman (AS) announced, *'I will not hear of anyone who says that the demons know the Unseen, but I will rather cut off his head.'*

When Prophet Suleiman (AS) passed away and the knowledgeable researchers and scholars who knew about the reality about Prophet Suleiman also died, another era was born. The devil disguised himself as a human and whispered to some of the Children of Israel, 'Should I lead you to a fortune that you will never have the capacity to go through?'

Lust tainted their eyes & they (the Children of Israel) said. 'Yes.'

He (the devil) stated, `Dig under this throne,' as he escorted them to the throne of the Prophet Suleiman (AS).

`Come closer.' the children of Israel iterated.

He (the devil) stated, `No. I will just wait for you here, and if you do not find the treasure, then kill me.

They dug and found the hidden books and Satan said to them, 'Suleiman manipulated the humans, devils, and birds with this magic.'

From that point onwards, the false news that Suleiman was a magician spread amongst the masses, deceiving the Children of Israel again who embraced these books.

Legend says that this is how black magic was first introduced into this world.

Story Number 3:

The Heifer

Al-Baqarah 67-73 add ayats

An old man from among the Children of Israel was very rich, and he had some nephews who wished he would die soon to inherit him. One day, one of them on purpose murdered him at night and threw him on the road -or at the door of one of his own brothers. In the morning, the people found the dead body and they disputed over him. His nephew -the murderer -came and began to weep and cry. Some people said: Why do you dispute him? Why do not you go to Allah's Prophet?

His nephew came and complained to Musa A.S. Musa A.S. said: by Allah! Anyone who knows anything about this murdered man, he should let us know. But, no one knew anything about it. Thereupon, they asked Musa A.S. to ask his Lord concerning this issue. Musa A.S. asked his Lord and he was commanded to order them to slaughter a cow.

About the cow to be slaughtered, Musa A.S. told them,

'It is a cow neither trained to tilt the soil nor water the fields, sound, having no other color except bright yellow.'

It is said that they could not find a cow with all these descriptions but with a man who was righteous and good to his father. They asked him to submit it to them, but he refused. They tried to seduce him as to its price till they offered him what equals its weight in gold. But, he refused. Then, they offered him an amount of gold that equals its weight ten-times. Finally, he accepted their offer and submitted it to them.

Then, Musa A.S. commanded them to slaughter it *(So they slaughtered it though they were near to not doing it)* i.e. they were hesitant.

Then, Musa A.S. instructed them with the Command of Allah to strike the dead man with a piece of the cow.

When they stroked him with the thigh bone of the cow, he was resurrected by Allah the Almighty. Musa A.S. asked him: Who's your murderer? He said: it was my nephew who killed me. Then, he died again.

Allah the Almighty says *(Thus Allah brings the dead to life and shows you His Ayat so that you may understand)* i.e. as you witnessed the revival of that dead man by the Command of Allah the Almighty, He can do the same to all the dead people when He wishes to.

Almighty Allah, says

The creation of you all and the resurrection of you all are only as (the creation and resurrection of) a single person. Verily, Allah is All-Hearer, All-Seer. (Luqman, 28)

Story Number 4:

Dwellers of the Town

13-27 surat yasin

إِذْ أَرْسَلْنَآ إِلَيْهِمُ ٱثْنَيْنِ فَكَذَّبُوهُمَا فَعَزَّزْنَا بِثَالِثٍ فَقَالُوٓا إِنَّا إِلَيْكُم مُّرْسَلُونَ ١٤

We sent them two messengers, but they rejected both. So We reinforced ˹the two˺ with a third, and they declared, "We have indeed been sent to you ˹as messengers˺."

قَالُوا مَا أَنتُمْ إِلَّا بَشَرٌ مِّثْلُنَا وَمَا أَنزَلَ ٱلرَّحْمَـٰنُ مِن شَىْءٍ إِنْ أَنتُمْ إِلَّا تَكْذِبُونَ ١٥

The people replied, "You are only humans like us, and the Most Compassionate has not revealed anything. You are simply lying!"

قَالُوا رَبُّنَا يَعْلَمُ إِنَّا إِلَيْكُمْ لَمُرْسَلُونَ ١٦

The messengers responded, "Our Lord knows that we have truly been sent to you.

وَمَا عَلَيْنَآ إِلَّا ٱلْبَلَـٰغُ ٱلْمُبِينُ ١٧

And our duty is only to deliver ˹the message˺ clearly."

قَالُوٓا إِنَّا تَطَيَّرْنَا بِكُمْ ۖ لَئِن لَّمْ تَنتَهُوا لَنَرْجُمَنَّكُمْ وَلَيَمَسَّنَّكُم مِّنَّا عَذَابٌ أَلِيمٌ ١٨

The people replied, "We definitely see you as a bad omen for us. If you do not desist, we will certainly stone

*you ˹to death˺ and you will be touched with a painful pun-
ishment from us."*

There was a town called Antioch, governed by the king
Antikhis Ibn Antikhis. This king used to observe idol worship. Allah Almighty sent him three Messengers whom he
severely believed.

The Messengers were: Sadiq, Masduq and Shalom.

Allah the Almighty says that O Muhammad! Put the
story of the dwellers of this town as an example for your
people. The people of the town said that the Messengers
were only human beings and they set aside the idea
that Allah Almighty might send human beings as His
Messengers to mankind.

People of the town threatened the messengers of
Allah with afflicting humiliation (bad words) and killing (stoning to death). People of the town said to the
messengers,'you are bad omen'

The messengers replied,'Your evil omens be with you!
Do you call it "evil omen " because we reminded you with
guidance and invited you to it? You threatened us with
killing and afflicting humiliation.

You do so because you transgress all bounds and
orders of the Almighty Allah.

And there came a man running from the farthest part
of the town to support the Messengers and to declare his

faith in them. *(He said: O my people! Obey the Messengers. Obey those who ask no wages of you (for themselves), and who are rightly guided)*

Then he invited them to worship Allah Alone, and not to worship other than Him that can do nothing in this present life or in the Hereafter.

Then, the believing man said to the three Messengers: Verily! I have believed in your Lord so you should listen to my statement and bear witness to this before your Lord. O my people! Listen to my declaration of faith of these Messengers.

Thereupon, the people killed him either by stoning him to death

When he was killed by his people, Allah Almighty admitted him into Paradise. When he saw the pleasures and joys therein, he said: {Would that my people knew? That my Lord (Allah) has forgiven me, and made me of the honored ones!}

Allah mentioned this story in the heart of the Quran, Surah al-Yasin, to narrate to the ummah, the punishment of disrespecting and not believing in the message and messenger of Allah.

Story Number 5

The Story of Uzair A.S.

Al-Baqarah 259

أَوْ كَٱلَّذِى مَرَّ عَلَىٰ قَرْيَةٍ وَهِيَ خَاوِيَةٌ عَلَىٰ عُرُوشِهَا قَالَ أَنَّىٰ يُحْىِۦ هَٰذِهِ ٱللَّهُ بَعْدَ مَوْتِهَا ۖ فَأَمَاتَهُ ٱللَّهُ مِائَةَ عَامٍ ثُمَّ بَعَثَهُۥ ۖ قَالَ كَمْ لَبِثْتَ ۖ قَالَ لَبِثْتُ يَوْمًا أَوْ بَعْضَ يَوْمٍ ۖ قَالَ بَل لَّبِثْتَ مِائَةَ عَامٍ فَٱنظُرْ إِلَىٰ طَعَامِكَ وَشَرَابِكَ لَمْ يَتَسَنَّهْ ۖ وَٱنظُرْ إِلَىٰ حِمَارِكَ وَلِنَجْعَلَكَ ءَايَةً لِّلنَّاسِ ۖ وَٱنظُرْ إِلَى ٱلْعِظَامِ كَيْفَ نُنشِزُهَا ثُمَّ نَكْسُوهَا لَحْمًا ۚ فَلَمَّا تَبَيَّنَ لَهُۥ قَالَ أَعْلَمُ أَنَّ ٱللَّهَ عَلَىٰ كُلِّ شَىْءٍ قَدِيرٌ ٢٥٩

Or ˹are you not aware of˺ the one who passed by a city which was in ruins. He wondered, "How could Allah bring this back to life after its destruction?" So Allah caused him to die for a hundred years then brought him back to life. Allah asked, "How long have you remained ˹in this state˺?" He replied, "Perhaps a day or part of a day." Allah said, "No! You have remained here for a hundred years! Just look at your food and drink—they have not spoiled. ˹But now˺ look at ˹the remains of˺ your donkey! And ˹so˺ We have made you into a sign for humanity. And look at the bones ˹of the donkey˺, how We bring them together then clothe them with flesh!" When this was made clear to him, he declared, "˹Now˺ I know that Allah is Most Capable of everything."

Uzair was a wise, pious worshiper. One day, he went out to look after some of his properties, when he finished he passed by a ruined place where he was scorched by the blazing sun. *So,* he entered that ruined place riding on his donkey. He got off the donkey holding two baskets, one full of figs and the other full of grapes. He sat down and brought out a bowl in which he squeezed the grapes and soaked the dried bread he had therein. He ate and then slept on his back, leaning his two legs against a wall and started to gaze at the ceiling of the house. He saw some decomposed bones and said: *(Oh! How will Allah ever bring it to life after its death!)* He did not doubt Allah's Omnipotence to do this, but he said it in exclamation.

Upon this, Allah the Almighty sent the Angel of Death who seized his soul, and thus Allah caused him to die for a hundred years. And, after one hundred years, Allah the Almighty sent to him an Angel who first created his heart to make him heedful, then, he created his two eyes to enable him to see and realize how Allah the Almighty revived the dead. Then, the Angel continued to complete his creation once more while he was looking. Then, he clothed his bones with flesh, skin and hair. Then, he breathed the soul into him. All this while he is looking and perfectly heedful. The Angel asked him saying: {How *long* did you *remain (dead)?* He *(the* man) said: *(Perhaps) I remained (dead)* a day or part of a day}

The Angel said: {Nay, you have *remained (dead)* for a hundred years, *look* at your *food* and your drink} i.e. the dried bread and the squeezed grapes that did not alter or turn bad, and the grapes and the figs did not change as well. As if he began to deny the matter by heart, the Angel said: do you deny what I have said? {and *look* at your *donkey!*} he looked at his donkey and found his bones to be decomposed and became totally ruined. The Angel called upon the donkey's bones and they answered his call and gathered together from all directions till he was made one whole again –while 'Uzair was looking and he clothed them with flesh, skin and hair. Then, the Angel breathed life into it and it roused erecting his ears and head towards the sky thinking the Last Hour had come.

Then, he rode on his donkey back to his village where he seemed unfamiliar to the people and the people looked unfamiliar to him. He did not find his own house easily. When he reached the house, he found a crippled blind old woman at the age of one hundred twenty years old. She was a maid owned by him in the past and he left her while she was only twenty years old. He asked her saying: is this the house of 'Uzair? She said: Yes, it is. She wept and said: Today, no one ever remembers 'Uzair.

He told her that he was 'Uzair and Allah the Almighty caused me to die for one hundred years then He gave me life again. She said: Glory is to be to Allah! We lost 'Uzair one hundred years ago and never heard anything about him. He said: Verily, I am 'Uzair. She said: 'Uzair was a man whose supplications were acceptable by Allah the Almighty, so invoke Allah to return my sight to me to look at you, so if you were 'Uzair, I would certainly know you. Consequently, he invoked Allah the Almighty, then, he wiped over her eyes and they were recovered and took her by the hand and said: Stand up by the Leave of Allah! She stood up by the Leave of Allah. She looked at him and said: I bear witness that you are 'Uzair. Then, she set out for the Children of Israel in their meetings and gatherings and Uzair's son who was about one hundred and eighteen years old and his grandsons, and she called them saying: This is 'Uzair who came back to you.

He was a sign for the people, as said by Allah the Almighty: *(And thus We have made of you a sign for the people)* i.e. for the Children of Israel. There he was, with his sons, a young man among old people for he died when he was only forty and was revived at the same age and status.

Story number 6:

The Story of the Sabbath

Al-Baqarah 65, 66

﴿وَلَقَدْ عَلِمْتُمُ الَّذِينَ اعْتَدَوْا مِنْكُمْ فِى السَّبْتِ فَقُلْنَا لَهُمْ كُوْنُوْا قِرَدَةً خَاسِـئِيْنَ ٢:٦٥﴾

And you know the case of those of you who broke the Sabbath,[82] how We said to them: "Become apes, despised and hated."

﴿فَجَعَلْنٰهَا نَكَالاً لِّمَا بَيْنَ يَدَيْهَا وَمَا خَلْفَهَا وَمَوْعِظَةً لِّلْمُتَّقِيْنَ ٢:٦٦﴾

And thus We made their end a warning for the people of their own time and for the succeeding generations, and an admonition to the God-fearing.

The people *of Aylah* were adhering attentively *to* the teachings *of* the Torah and the prohibition *of* the Sabbath at that time (the prohibition *of* fishing on Saturdays). Amazingly, the fish used *to* expose itself openly on Saturdays and disappear on the other days *of* the week, *(when their fish came to them openly on the Sabbath day, and did not come to them on the day they had no Sabbath).* Almighty Allah says *(Thus We made a trial of them),* i.e. We test them through sending great numbers *of* fish on the Sabbath. *(for they used to rebel against Allah's Command (disobey Allah)),* i.e. because *of* their disobedience and rebellion. When they saw this, they made a trick *to* catch the fish on the Sabbath.

They fixed their fishing nets and ropes and excavated streams allowing the sea water *to* run through and the fish *to* get in but never *go* back *to* the sea. They made all this on Friday, in preparation *for* the coming *of* the fish on Saturday. And thus, the fish came on the supposedly-peaceful day.

When the Saturday came *to* an end, the people *of Aylah* were present *to* take their fat catch. Consequently, Allah the Almighty was angry with them and He cursed them because *of* their trickery and deception.

When this was done by a group thereof, the rest who did *not* participate in their sinful acting were divided into two sects: a sect that rejected their acting and trickery against the Law and Command *of* Allah the Almighty at that time. The second sect did *not* reject or forbid them, rather they disapproved *of* the reaction *of* the sect that forbade the sinful ones.

Allah the Almighty informed us that He destroyed the wrong-doers, saved the preaching believers and left the believers who did not practice enjoining the good and forbidding the evil. Scholars disputed the third group. Some said they were granted salvation. And others said that they were destroyed with the wrong-doers.

It should be noted here that the third group were not mentioned with those given salvation even though they despised the sinful deed, with their hearts, because they should have compelled their organs (hand or tongue) to act thereupon and declare their rejection of the wrong-doers' act.

Story Number 7:

Maryam A.S. : The Single Mother

Surah al-tahrim 33-35

إِنَّ ٱللَّهَ ٱصْطَفَىٰٓ ءَادَمَ وَنُوحًا وَءَالَ إِبْرَٰهِيمَ وَءَالَ عِمْرَٰنَ عَلَى ٱلْعَٰلَمِينَ ٣٣ ﴿۞﴾

Indeed, Allah chose Adam, Noah, the family of Abraham, and the family of 'Imrân above all people ˹of their time˺.

ذُرِّيَّةَۢ بَعْضُهَا مِنۢ بَعْضٍ ۗ وَٱللَّهُ سَمِيعٌ عَلِيمٌ ٣٤

They are descendants of one another. And Allah is All-Hearing, All-Knowing.

إِذْ قَالَتِ ٱمْرَأَتُ عِمْرَٰنَ رَبِّ إِنِّى نَذَرْتُ لَكَ مَا فِى بَطْنِى مُحَرَّرًا فَتَقَبَّلْ مِنِّىٓ ۖ إِنَّكَ أَنتَ ٱلسَّمِيعُ ٱلْعَلِيمُ ٣٥

˹Remember˺ when the wife of 'Imrân said, "My Lord! I dedicate what is in my womb entirely to Your service, so accept it from me. You ˹alone˺ are truly the All-Hearing, All-Knowing."

Maryam, mother of Hazrat Isa R.A. is the only woman mentioned by name in the Quran, raising her status as a chosen servant of Allah. A whole chapter bears her name, another is dedicated to her family, and her story is related in countless verses.

The birth of Maryam, may Allah be pleased with her, was a miracle in and of itself. Her mother, Hannah, wanted desperately to have a baby, so she supplicated and proposed that, should she become pregnant, she would offer the baby to the service of Allah. She hoped to have a male child that could be raised working in the mosque, Bait-ul-Maqdis. Hannah was later surprised when she gave birth to a girl. This story is told in detail in Surah Al-Imran, the chapter named after the family of Imran.

Ibn Kathir wrote that whenever she was not busy looking after the masjid, she would spend her time in solitude praying and supplicating to Allah. She had a private room built for her in the masjid and in the Quran it mentions that Allah used to send fruits that were out of season to her. Whenever Zakariya would check up on her, he used to see this food and ask where she had gotten it. She would respond, as it says in the Quran,

"It is from Allah, surely Allah bestows sustenance upon Whom He pleases without measure."
(Surah Al-Imran, 3:37)

Maryam, who was a young lady, no more than 15-years-old, received a visit from a group of angels, while she was in her private prayer room. This room was a sanctuary, and no men would ever enter save for Prophet Zakariyya, peace be upon him. Imagine Maryam's surprise when these strangers came in for a visit in human form.

Allah narrates this story in the Quran,

"When the angels said: 'O Mary! Allah gives you glad tidings of a Word from Him, his name is the Messiah Jesus, the son of Mary, held in honor in this world and in the Hereafter, and of those nearest to Allah. He shall speak to the people when in the cradle and in manhood, and he shall be from the righteous.' She said: 'My Lord! How can I have a son when no man has touched me?' He said: 'Even so, Allah creates what He pleases. When He decrees a matter, He says to it: Be – and it is. And He will teach him the Book and the wisdom, and the Torah and the Gospel.'" (Surah Al-Imran, 3:45-48)

Muhammad ibn Ishaaq said: "When she became pregnant with him and her menses ceased, and she experienced the discomforts that all pregnant women face, then no household experienced what the household of Zakariyah experienced. Talk (slander and gossip) spread among the Children of Israel... So, she stayed away from people and put a screen between her and them so that no one could see her, and she could not see anyone."

Maryam A.S. eventually gives birth to Isa A.S., and is commanded to take a vow of silence. Maryam would have still been recovering from childbirth, but she carries the baby back to her town to face the wrath of her people. Although she knew that people would begin to blame her, and she could possibly be punished for allegedly having a baby out of wedlock, Maryam still obeys Allah. Then, an incredible thing happens. Prophet Isa, performs his first miracle by the command of his Lord – he speaks as a newborn baby to defend his mother's innocence. Allah says about this incident,

"And We made the son of Mary and his mother a sign."
(Surah Al-Muminun, 23:50)

Throughout the Quran, Prophet Isa, peace be upon him, is called Isa ibn Maryam, Jesus, the son of Mary. In Surah Maryam, one of the things baby Isa says is that Allah has made him dutiful to his mother. There is no mention of father or family. This implies that she was his only parent and responsibility. Maryam would continue living her life as a single mother and virgin according to the Islamic tradition. Not only is she held in high esteem in the Muslim world, but also in Christianity.

Nowadays, single parents are often ostracized in the Islamic community. We should respect and support the dedicated, practicing parents who are raising righteous believers alone. It may be that their sacrifice earns them a favorable status with Allah, inshaAllah.

Story Number 8:

Musa meets Khidr

Surah al-kahf 65-68

فَوَجَدَا عَبْدًا مِّنْ عِبَادِنَآ ءَاتَيْنَـٰهُ رَحْمَةً مِّنْ عِندِنَا وَعَلَّمْنَـٰهُ مِن لَّدُنَّا عِلْمًا ٦٥

There they found a servant of Ours, to whom We had granted mercy from Us and enlightened with knowledge of Our Own.

قَالَ لَهُۥ مُوسَىٰ هَلْ أَتَّبِعُكَ عَلَىٰٓ أَن تُعَلِّمَنِ مِمَّا عُلِّمْتَ رُشْدًا ٦٦

Moses said to him, "May I follow you, provided that you teach me some of the right guidance you have been taught?"

قَالَ إِنَّكَ لَن تَسْتَطِيعَ مَعِىَ صَبْرًا ٦٧

He said, "You certainly cannot be patient ˹enough˺ with me.

وَكَيْفَ تَصْبِرُ عَلَىٰ مَا لَمْ تُحِطْ بِهِۦ خُبْرًا ٦٨

And how can you be patient with what is beyond your realm of knowledge?

One day, Musa delivered such an impressive sermon that all who heard it were deeply moved. Someone in the congregation asked: *"O Messenger of Allah, is there another man on earth more learned than you?"* Musa replied:

22

"*No!*", believing so, as Allah had given him the power of miracles and honored him with the Torat.

However, Allah revealed to Musa that no man could know all there is to know, nor would one messenger alone be the custodian of all knowledge. There would always be another who knew what others did not.

Musa asked Allah: "*O Allah, where is this man who knows more than me? I would like to meet him and learn from him.*"

Allah instructed him to take a dead fish in a water-filled vessel. Where the fish disappeared, he would find the man he sought. Musa set out on his journey, accompanied by a young man. They reached a place where two rivers met and decided to rest there. Instantly, Musa fell asleep.

While he was asleep, his companion saw the dead fish come back to life and wriggle out of the vessel into the river and swim away! However, he forgot to relate this incident to Musa. When he awoke, they continued their journey. Musa asked for his morning meal. Only then did his companion tell him that the fish they had brought with them had gotten away. Hearing this, Musa exclaimed: "We have to go back there!"

There they found a man. His get-up showed he was a saintly man. He was Al-Khidr, the guide.

Musa said to him (Khidr) "May I follow you so that you teach me something of that knowledge (guidance and true path) which you have been taught (by Allah)?"

He (Khidr) said: "Verily! You will not be able to have patience with me! And how can you have patience about a thing which you know not?"

Musa said: "If Allah will, you will find me patient, and I will not disobey you in aught."

He (Khidr) said: "Then, if you follow me, ask me not about anything till I myself mention it to you."

So they both proceeded, till, when they were in the ship, he (Khidr) scuttled it by making a hole in it. Musa said: "Have you scuttled it in order to drown its people? Verily, you have done Imra - a Munkar (evil, bad, dreadful) thing."

He (Khidr) said: "Did I not tell you, that you would not be able to have patience with me?"

(Musa) said: "Call me not to account for what I forgot, and be not hard upon me for my affair."

Then they both proceeded, till they met a boy, Khidr killed him. Musa said: "Have you killed an innocent person who had killed none? Verily, you have done Nukra a great Munkar (prohibited, evil, dreadful) thing!"

Khidr said: "Did I not tell you that you can have no patience with me?"

Musa said: "If I ask you anything after this, keep me not in your company, you have received an excuse from me."

Then they both proceeded, till, when they came to the people of a town, they asked them for food, but they refused to entertain them. Then they found therein a wall about to collapse and he (Khidr) set it up straight. Musa said: "If you had wished, surely you could have taken wages for it!"

For Musa, it was a bit unnecessary for Khizr to repair that wall with his own hands when the people of the town did not even give them food. He also pointed out that you could take wages for this job so that we could buy some food for ourselves.

At Musa questioning for the third time, Khizr parted ways with him.

Khidr said: "This is the parting between me and you. I will tell you the interpretation of (those) things over which you were unable to hold patience.

'As for the ship, it belonged to poor people working in the sea. So I wished to make a defective damage in it, as there was a king after them who seized every ship by force.

"And as for the boy, his parents were believers, and we feared lest he should oppress them by rebellion and disbelief. So we intended that their Lord should change him for them for the one better in righteousness and near to mercy.

"And as for the wall, it belonged to two orphan boys in the town; and there was under it a treasure belonging to them; and their father was a righteous man, and your Lord intended that they should attain their age of full strength and take out their treasure as a mercy from your Lord. And I did it not of my own accord. That is the interpretation of those (things) over which you could not hold patience. "

Quran Ayah 18:60-82

Story Number 9:

The Pleading Woman

Surah al-Mujadalah 1-3

قَدْ سَمِعَ ٱللَّهُ قَوْلَ ٱلَّتِى تُجَـٰدِلُكَ فِى زَوْجِهَا وَتَشْتَكِىٓ إِلَى ٱللَّهِ وَٱللَّهُ يَسْمَعُ تَحَاوُرَكُمَآ ۚ إِنَّ ٱللَّهَ سَمِيعٌۢ بَصِيرٌ ١

Certainly has Allah heard the speech of the one who argues with you, [O Muhammad], concerning her husband and directs her complaint to Allah . And Allah hears your dialogue; indeed, Allah is Hearing and Seeing.

أَلَّذِينَ يُظَٰهِرُونَ مِنكُم مِّن نِّسَآئِهِم مَّا هُنَّ أُمَّهَٰتِهِمْ ۖ إِنْ أُمَّهَٰتُهُمْ إِلَّا ٱلَّٰٓـِٔى وَلَدْنَهُمْ ۚ
وَإِنَّهُمْ لَيَقُولُونَ مُنكَرًا مِّنَ ٱلْقَوْلِ وَزُورًا ۚ وَإِنَّ ٱللَّهَ لَعَفُوٌّ غَفُورٌ ٢

*Those who pronounce thihar among you [to separate]
from their wives – they are not [consequently] their mothers. Their mothers are none but those who gave birth to
them. And indeed, they are saying an objectionable statement and a falsehood. But indeed, Allah is Pardoning and
Forgiving.*

وَٱلَّذِينَ يُظَٰهِرُونَ مِن نِّسَآئِهِمْ ثُمَّ يَعُودُونَ لِمَا قَالُوا۟ فَتَحْرِيرُ رَقَبَةٍ مِّن قَبْلِ أَن يَتَمَآسَّا ۚ
ذَٰلِكُمْ تُوعَظُونَ بِهِۦ ۚ وَٱللَّهُ بِمَا تَعْمَلُونَ خَبِيرٌ ٣

*And those who pronounce thihar from their wives and
then [wish to] go back on what they said – then [there must
be] the freeing of a slave before they touch one another.
That is what you are admonished thereby; and Allah is
Acquainted with what you do.*

(Holy Quran, 58: 1-3)

Khaula was married to Aws ibn As-Samit. One day
they had an argument. Aws divorced her by "Thihar," a
pagan custom of divorcing a wife by saying, "Be to me as
my mother's back."

Khaula decided to go to the prophet of Allah for jus-
tice. She entered the hujra of Hazrat Ayesha R.A., where
she was oiling and combing the hair of the Prophet
Muhammad SAW. She told him everything, to which

prophet PBUH responded that Oh Khaula! You are forbidden for your husband now.

She pleaded again, asking the prophet of Allah to please reconsider.

'I am old, I cannot remarry. My kids are young, I cannot feed them. Please have some mercy, Rasool Allah SAW.'

Prophet Muhammad SAW said again,

'Oh Khaula! You are forbidden for your husband now.'

Khaula, crying and wailing, then went to Allah, the Master of Prophet Muhammad SAW, and made dua.

Allah responded to her prayer by revealing the first four verses of Surah Al Mujadila, "The Pleading Woman", and rejected zihar forever.

Allah preceded the pleading woman over His prophet. SUBHANALLAH

Story Number 10:

Qarun

Surah al-qasas 79, 80

فَخَرَجَ عَلَىٰ قَوْمِهِۦ فِى زِينَتِهِۦۖ قَالَ ٱلَّذِينَ يُرِيدُونَ ٱلْحَيَوٰةَ ٱلدُّنْيَا يَٰلَيْتَ لَنَا مِثْلَ مَآ أُوتِىَ قَٰرُونُ إِنَّهُۥ لَذُو حَظٍّ عَظِيمٍ ٧٩

Then he came out before his people in all his glamor. Those who desired the life of this world wished, "If only we could have something like what Korah has been given. He is truly a man of great fortune!"

وَقَالَ ٱلَّذِينَ أُوتُوا۟ ٱلْعِلْمَ وَيْلَكُمْ ثَوَابُ ٱللَّهِ خَيْرٌ لِّمَنْ ءَامَنَ وَعَمِلَ صَٰلِحًا وَلَا يُلَقَّىٰهَآ إِلَّا ٱلصَّٰبِرُونَ ٨٠

But those gifted with knowledge said, "Shame on you! Allah's reward is far better for those who believe and do good. But none will attain this except the steadfast."

Qaaroon was a cousin of Hazrat musa. He was a very handsome young man, who also had pleasant manners. He apparently accepted the shariat of musa a.s and also read torat. In fact, he was one of the scholars of torat. But he was a person of weak iman. He had greed for money and power. He used to buy grain and crops and then sell them at higher prices. Lending money for huge inter-est rates was his business. Slowly and eventually he had accumulated so much wealth that he had treasures of gold and jewels.

Qaaroon had hundreds of camels who used to wear jewels. The keys of his treasure alone had to be mounted on various camels. He had become arrogant and cruel. People would bow down in front of him and envy his good luck and luxurious life.

One day, Allah sent the orders of zakat to Hazrat musa A.S. Hazrat Musa told Qaaroon about the order of zakat. The revelation also told the people that Allah does not like the proud and those who cause fitna on the earth.

In Surah al-qasas, this advice from Allah has been mentioned as:

"And seek by means of what Allah has given you, the abode of the Hereafter, and do not forget your portion in this world, and be good (to others) just as Allah has been good to you, and do not seek to make mischief in the land, verily Allah does not love the mischief-makers."

To this, qaroon disobeyed. He refused to pay the zakat, saying whoever wants money, should earn it himself.

Hazrat Musa argued that if it was not for these poor laborers, you would not have earned all these riches.

He said, o musa! Is this a crime that we believe in Allah and act upon your shariat? Is it a crime that we pray to Allah and fast for Him? Why do you charge us for that?

Though he finally agreed to pay the zakat. But when he calculated the amount, it was a huge chunk of his treasure. He downright disobeyed the hukm of Allah. Not just that, he planned to defame hazrat musa. He told the people of bani Israel that Hazrat Musa wants to rob you in the name of Allah and take all your money away.

Not only that, Qaroon prepared a plan to allegate Musa in a case of adultery. He paid a woman a huge amount of money and told her to allege Hazrat musa and tell everyone that He has had physical relationship with her without marriage.

Hazrat Musa was giving a sermon when Qaarun interrupted him and said:

"Children of Israel say you committed adultery with such and such a woman."

Hazrat Musa said, "Call that woman here. If she says so, it is true."

They called the woman and she came. Hazrat Musa asked her, "Did you commit adultery with me as they claim?"

The woman got terrified of the strong personality and she said,

"No. They are lying. They gave me a lot of money so that I will slander you." Musa prostrated in the sujood of shukr immediately.

Allah Almighty sent a revelation to Musa and said, "Today, I have put the earth under your command; you can order it as you wish."

Musa ordered the earth,

"Swallow him!" The earth started to swallow him. As he gave each order, the earth swallowed more and more. First, the earth swallowed him up to his knees, then to his waist and then his neck. Qaarun begged Musa for mercy.

Musa was a hot-blooded man and continued giving orders. Finally, Qaaron disappeared into the earth.

After that Musa ordered the earth to swallow the wealth, the castles, and the treasures of Qaroon.

In Surah Al-Qasas 28:76, Allah has talked about the riches of qaroon:

'To be sure, Qarun (Korah) was one of Musa's people; then he transgressed against them. We had bestowed on him such treasure that their very keys would have been raised with difficulty by a whole group of strong people.'

This is how a handsome, beautiful, soft-spoken man came to an end. Not because he was a disbeliever. He was in fact a believer and a scholar of torat. He suffered his punishment because he spread fitna and wrong allegations about a pious man of Allah. He was proud and arrogant, and he forgot his place in front of Allah.

Story Number 10:

The Queen of Sheba

Al-Naml 20-44

قَالَتْ يَـٰٓأَيُّهَا ٱلْمَلَؤُاْ إِنِّىٓ أُلْقِىَ إِلَىَّ كِتَـٰبٌ كَرِيمٌ ٢٩

The Queen ˹later˺ announced, "O chiefs! Indeed, a noble letter has been delivered to me.

إِنَّهُ مِن سُلَيْمَـٰنَ وَإِنَّهُۥ بِسْمِ ٱللَّهِ ٱلرَّحْمَـٰنِ ٱلرَّحِيمِ ٣٠

It is from Solomon, and it reads: 'In the Name of Allah—the Most Compassionate, Most Merciful.

أَلَّا تَعْلُواْ عَلَىَّ وَأْتُونِى مُسْلِمِينَ ٣١

Do not be arrogant with me, but come to me, fully submitting ˹to Allah.'"

قَالَتْ يَـٰٓأَيُّهَا ٱلْمَلَؤُاْ أَفْتُونِى فِى أَمْرِى مَا كُنتُ قَاطِعَةً أَمْرًا حَتَّىٰ تَشْهَدُونِ ٣٢

She said, "O chiefs! Advise me in this matter of mine, for I would never make any decision without you."

All kinds of birds had pioneers or chosen ones who were charged with certain tasks and who periodically attended themselves before Sulaiman, as a habit of the troops with their kings. The mission of the hoopoe was to search for water in deserts and barren areas.

One day one of the Hoopoes narrated to Suleman, a unique incident. He describes the status of the kings and rulers of Sheba in Yemen: they had a mighty and glorious kingdom along with strong and competent troops. During that period, their king died and left no heirs but a daughter whom they raised as their queen.

The Queen of Sheba, known by the name Bilqis, had everything a ruler could own. The chair she sits on was ornamented and studded with various jewels, pearls, gold and other magnificent things. Then, he mentioned their disbelief in Allah the Almighty and their worship of the sun instead of Allah and the deceivement of Satan to them by making their deeds look fair-seeming in their eyes, and barring them from Allah's Way.

Thereupon, Sulaiman sent the hoopoe with a letter calling them to obey Allah and His Messenger, to repent and submit themselves to his kingship and power. He sent them: *(Be you not exalted against me)* i. e. do not let your pride prevent you from obeying me, *(but come to me as Muslims)* i.e. true believers who submit to Allah with full submission.

The hoopoe dropped the letter near her and waited to see what she was going to do. However, she gathered the nobles, princes and ministers to have mutual consultation,

The chiefs expressed confidence in their strong army's proficiency in the case of a war. She wisely opted against going to war after considering how calamitous it could be for her nation. Instead, she sent some men with gifts to the Prophet Sulaiman (AS) to see how he would answer.

The messengers took the gifts to Sulaiman's palace and personally witnessed his formidable army and tremendous affluence.

Sulaiman said to the chief of her messengers who brought the present; go back with your gifts for what I have been granted by Allah is far better than these properties, riches and presents with which you rejoice and be filled with arrogance and pride over your own people.

This was a warning that if Bilqis did not comply, the strongest army on Earth would perish Sheba.

When they heard the news, they rushed declaring their full submission and perfect obedience and willingness to accompany their queen in her leaving for meeting Sulaiman. When he heard of their coming and their intention to present themselves before his hand, he asked a jinn to bring him her throne before she came.

The throne of Bilqis was brought and placed before him, in this too short period, from the Yemen to Jerusalem,

Then, Sulaiman (Peace be upon him) ordered her throne to be altered and disguised to test her mentality and understanding.

When the Queen was made to enter the palace, she confused the floor with water. So, to enter the palace, she lifted her dress.

(But when she saw it, she thought it was a pool, and she (tucked up her clothes) uncovered her legs. (Sulaiman) said: "Verily, it is a Sarh (a glass surface with water underneath it or a palace)."

At last she submitted before Allah and the truth. Allah says in Surah Al-Naml,

'She said: "My Lord! Verily, I have wronged myself, and I submit [in Islam, together with Sulaiman (Solomon)). to Allah, the Lord of the" Alamin (mankind, jinn and all that exists)).'

Bilqis finds peace in her heart when she submits to God. It is such a simple thing to do, yet for many, it is one of the most difficult. The story of the visit to Solomon by the Queen of Sheba is meant to teach us that submitting to God is richer than silver or gold, and better than splendor or wealth.

Story Number 11:

The People of Saba

Surat Saba' 15-19

لَقَدْ كَانَ لِسَبَإٍ فِى مَسْكَنِهِمْ ءَايَةٌ ۖ جَنَّتَانِ عَن يَمِينٍ وَشِمَالٍ ۖ كُلُوا۟ مِن رِّزْقِ رَبِّكُمْ وَٱشْكُرُوا۟ لَهُۥ ۚ بَلْدَةٌ طَيِّبَةٌ وَرَبٌّ غَفُورٌ ١٥

Indeed, there was a sign for ʿthe tribe ofʾ Sheba in their homeland: two orchards—one to the right and the other to the left. ʿThey were told:ʾ "Eat from the provision of your Lord, and be grateful to Him. ʿYours isʾ a good land and a forgiving Lord."

فَأَعْرَضُوا۟ فَأَرْسَلْنَا عَلَيْهِمْ سَيْلَ ٱلْعَرِمِ وَبَدَّلْنَـٰهُم بِجَنَّتَيْهِمْ جَنَّتَيْنِ ذَوَاتَىْ أُكُلٍ خَمْطٍ وَأَثْلٍ وَشَىْءٍ مِّن سِدْرٍ قَلِيلٍ ١٦

But they turned away. So We sent against them a devastating flood, and replaced their orchards with two others producing bitter fruit, fruitless bushes, and a few ʿsparseʾ thorny trees.

ذَٰلِكَ جَزَيْنَـٰهُم بِمَا كَفَرُوا۟ ۖ وَهَلْ نُجَـٰزِىٓ إِلَّا ٱلْكَفُورَ ١٧

This is how We rewarded them for their ingratitude. Would We ever punish ʿanyone in such a wayʾ except the ungrateful?

The people of Saba' were the kings of Yemen and Balqees, the wife of Sulayman A.S. was from them. The people of Saba' lived happy and joyful lives that were full of blessings; their sustenance was abundant and their trees and plants very fruitful. Allah sent messengers to them, instructing them to eat from what He had provided for them and show gratitude towards Him, as well as to worship Him alone and believe in His oneness. They adhered to these instructions for a while, but then shunned His commandments, and were thus punished by a flood on their land.

Ibn 'Abbas R.A. narrated that a man came to the Prophet SAW and asked him whether Saba' was a name of a man, a woman or a land; the Prophet SAW answered: *"It is the name of a man who had ten children from his progeny, all of whom were Arab; six of them later lived in Yemen and four in Sham* (modern Syria and including some other surrounding nations). *The ones in Yemen were later known as the tribes of Mathhij, Kindah, Al-Azd, Al-Asha'iriyyoon, Anmar and Himyar. As for the ones who lived in Sham, they were to be the known tribes of Lakhm, Jutham, 'Aamilah and Ghassan."*[Ahmad]

The sign that Allah gave to them refers to their land, which was blessed with fields of gardens, as well as being protected from afflictions, all of which necessitated gratitude. These gardens yielded enough fruits to suffice them, so they were overwhelmed by the happiness of being free from need. Allah commanded them to express gratitude for these favors, namely:

1. The abundant provision He provided for them from these two gardens.
2. Good land and a beautiful climate
3. The forgiveness they were promised in return for expressing gratitude towards Allah.

Instead of continuing to be thankful, they turned away and shunned the commandments of Allah; they shunned Tawheed and His worship, and refused to be thankful; they began worshiping the sun instead of Allah.

The flood that Allah sent upon them comprised a huge amount of water, which resulted in the total destruction of their gardens; their fruitful trees were rendered into others that were useless, bearing bitter fruits.

Look what happened to them! Look how their gardens, with their fruitful trees, pleasant shade and fine natural views, were rendered into thorns and trees with bitter fruits, all of which resulted from their ungratefulness, their refusal of the truth and their association with Allah. What was the result? *"...That We repaid them"* meaning that they were punished.

People of the Cave

Surat al-kahf 9-26

أَمْ حَسِبْتَ أَنَّ أَصْحَٰبَ ٱلْكَهْفِ وَٱلرَّقِيمِ كَانُوا۟ مِنْ ءَايَٰتِنَا عَجَبًا ٩

Have you ˹O Prophet˺ thought that the people of the cave and the plaque 1 were ˹the only˺ wonders of Our signs?

إِذْ أَوَى ٱلْفِتْيَةُ إِلَى ٱلْكَهْفِ فَقَالُوا۟ رَبَّنَآ ءَاتِنَا مِن لَّدُنكَ رَحْمَةً وَهَيِّئْ لَنَا مِنْ أَمْرِنَا رَشَدًا ١٠

˹Remember˺ when those youths took refuge in the cave, and said, "Our Lord! Grant us mercy from Yourself and guide us rightly through our ordeal."

فَضَرَبْنَا عَلَىٰٓ ءَاذَانِهِمْ فِى ٱلْكَهْفِ سِنِينَ عَدَدًا ١١

So We caused them to fall into a dead sleep in the cave for many years.

The people of Quraish sent to the Jews asking them for things to test the Prophet SAW with. The Jews said: ask him about a group of people who disappeared in the past and none has any knowledge about them. That is when these ayats of surah-al kahf were revealed, narrating a beautiful story filled with lessons and truth of the power of the Almighty.

A king named "Duqyânus" ordered the people in his territory "Afsus" (nowadays Turkey) to worship the idols.

One day one of the disciples of `Isâ, `alayhi s-salam, visited that city. This man was a Muslim calling to the Religion of Islam.

Later on, this disciple became acquainted with some youngsters in the city. He taught them the knowledge of Oneness of Allah and about deeming Him clear of having a child, possessing a form, or being designated with a place. He invited them to Islam. They believed in Allah and converted to Islam. They practiced the Religion and followed its rules.

The story of those youngsters, who became devoted to the Religion of Islam and to the worship of Allah alone, became well known. The king was informed about them and was told, "Those people left your religion, and mocked and defied your idols." The king called them to his court and ordered them to leave Islam. He threatened them with killing if they declined.

He claimed that they were young and they did not have a mature mind. Hence, he did not want to kill them immediately. Instead he wanted to give them enough time to think before he would carry out his threat. Then he sent them back to their homes.

In the meantime, King Duqyânus traveled. Those young men took advantage of his departure and consulted each other about running away to rescue their faith in their Religion.

One of them said, "I know a cave in the mountain. My father used to secure the sheep in it. Let us go there and hide until Allah grants us victory." They all agreed to that idea.

They went outside playing and rolling the ball in front of them so that nobody would notice them. Then they fled.

A barking dog named "QiTmir" followed them. Worried that non-believers might hear this barking and know of their place, they threw stones at the dog and pushed it away more than once. Every time the dog returned. At the end the dog raised its front paws up to the sky as if making supplication. With the help of Allah, it said, "O people! Why are you driving me away, why are you hitting me? Do not be scared of me. I do not disbelieve in Allah."

As a result, the young men were certain that Allah, by His Mercy, would protect them from harm. They sought refuge with Allah, and made dua to Him and said, "O Allah, grant us Mercy from You, and prepare (create) good matters for us."

They continued walking until they reached the cave. There they found fruits and water. They ate and drank. Then they lay down to rest.

A few moments later, they felt sleepy. Their heads dropped down and they slept heavily on the floor with their eyes open. Night after day, years passed one after the other and the young men were in slumber; sound asleep. They were prevented from hearing anything.

The gust of the wind would not annoy them and the rumble of the thunder would not awaken them. When the sun rose it did not hit them with its high heat, as a sign of their rank. When rising, it moved to the right of the cave; and when setting, it passed by its left.

Because their eyes were wide open, if one were to look at them, one would think them awake. In reality, they were heavy with sleep. Their eyes were left open, because it was better for their eyes to be exposed to the air so that they would not get impaired with lengthy closure.

It was also narrated that an honorable angel was in charge of turning them around. They were turned on their left and right sides twice a year, so their bodies would not decay. If one was to look at them, one would be frightened by them and run away. People could not see them and could not approach them.

After three hundred nine years of sleep, Allah woke them up. They could not stand the hunger they had. They asked one another about the length of the stay. One of them said, "We stayed one or less than a day."

Another one said, "We went to sleep this morning and now the sun is getting ready to set." The fourth one said, "Let us stop wondering. Allah knows best how long we stayed. Anyhow, let us send one of us with some money to bring us some food. That person must be alert and smart. No one should recognize him, or else he would be followed. Then King Duqyânus and his followers would be told. They would know of our place and would inflict various types of torture on us until they deviate us from our Religion."

After the hundreds of years that had passed, King Duqyânus passed away. A pious Muslim king replaced him.

The people of the city at that time were in disagreement regarding the gathering and resurrection of the bodies. Some people had doubts about it, and thought that it was very unlikely. They said that only souls would be gathered. However, the bodies will decay in the soil. Some of them said, "But body and soul will be equally resurrected."

The king became distressed and a quarrel was about to happen. So he made a supplication to ask Allah to make showing the proof of the truth easy.

At the time, Amlîkhâ, one of the men in the cave who was sent in search of food,

Reached the city of "Afsus". He was fearful and watchful. The changes in the landmarks and the structure of the buildings surprised him. That area used to be an open land for the sheep to graze; now there were high castles. Other castles had collapsed. There were scenes he was not familiar with and faces he did not recognize.

His eyes glanced unstable; he looked confused and hesitant. Someone turned around and asked him, "Are you a stranger to this city, and what are you looking for?"

He said, "I am not a stranger and I am looking for food to buy. I did not find the place where I used to buy food."

The man held his hand and took him to the owner of the restaurant. Amlîkhâ took his money out and gave it to the seller. The seller wondered, because the money had the picture of King Duqyânus on it. That king died three hundred or more years before. He thought Amlîkhâ discovered a treasure and that he had a wealth of money in his possession. People gathered around Amlîkhâ and took him to the righteous king.

The news of Amlîkhâ reached the king before his own arrival. The king was in fact waiting for him eagerly, because he had heard the story of the youngsters from his grandfather. When Amlikhâ came, the king asked him about his story. So Amlîkhâ told him what happened to him and his friends.

The king was pleased with that and said to his people, "Certainly, Allah sent you a sign to show the truth about what you differ."

The king, along with the people of the city, walked with Amlîkhâ. When they approached the cave, Amlîkhâ said, "I will go inside first so that my friends do not get scared." He went inside and informed his friends of what happened. He told them that King Duqyânus passed away and that the present king was a pious Muslim.

And went outside, greeted the king, then they went back into their cave. When the people who doubted resurrection saw them, they gave up their incorrect belief and believed that the correct conviction is that the gathering of people on the Day of Judgment happens by both body and soul.

Allah made it for people a reminder, a lesson, and a proof of His Great Power.

Allah has Power over everything.

Story Number 13:

The Believer and the Disbeliever

Surah al kahf 32-44

لَّٰكِنَّا۠ هُوَ ٱللَّهُ رَبِّى وَلَآ أُشْرِكُ بِرَبِّىٓ أَحَدًا ٣٨

But as for me: He is Allah, my Lord, and I will never associate anyone with my Lord ˹in worship˺.

وَلَوْلَآ إِذْ دَخَلْتَ جَنَّتَكَ قُلْتَ مَا شَآءَ ٱللَّهُ لَا قُوَّةَ إِلَّا بِٱللَّهِ ۚ إِن تَرَنِ أَنَا۠ أَقَلَّ مِنكَ مَالًا وَوَلَدًا ٣٩

If only you had said, upon entering your property, 'This is what Allah has willed! There is no power except with Allah!' Even though you see me inferior to you in wealth and offspring,

فَعَسَىٰ رَبِّىٓ أَن يُؤْتِيَنِ خَيْرًا مِّن جَنَّتِكَ وَيُرْسِلَ عَلَيْهَا حُسْبَانًا مِّنَ ٱلسَّمَآءِ فَتُصْبِحَ صَعِيدًا زَلَقًا ٤٠

perhaps my Lord will grant me ˹something˺ better than your garden, and send down upon your garden a thunderbolt from the sky, turning it into a barren waste.

Some scholars say that this story explained in the Quran is only an example that has not necessarily taken place in real life. But, the majority of scholars hold that it really took place and happened in this present life of ours.

It is well-known that one of these two men was a believer, while the other was a disbeliever. Each one of them was very rich. The believer spent all his riches and wealth in the Cause of Allah. On the other hand, the disbeliever, though granted gardens and orchards, diverted from Allah's Path. His two gardens contained grapes and date-palms surrounding his plants and grapes, along with overflowing rivers and water streams running everywhere along with his property. These two gardens have been mentioned in detail in the glorious Quran. The fruits of his trees and plants were numerous and count-less (only by Allah's Grace), and the sight of his gardens was very pleasant. However, the owner of the two gardens became proud and arrogant with the believing man say-ing: {I *am more than you in wealth and stronger in respect of men)*, as you spent all your wealth in vain and you did not do as I did: buying gardens and orchards and invest-ing the money to gain the profits later. You should have followed my very steps!

And, *(he went into his garden while in a state (of pride and disbelief), unjust to himself)*, in a state that is not pleasing to Allah the Almighty (with pride and arro-gance). And he *(said:* I *think not that this will ever perish)*, that is because there are plenty of its plants and trees and if any of these were to perish, he would certainly (as he thought) get it replaced with a better and more fine one. He thought he had everything: plentiful water, countless fruits, and varieties of plants.

Then, the disbeliever said: *(And* I *think not the Hour will ever come)*, as he put his perfect trust in the vain pleasures of this life of ours and belied the existence of the everlasting Hereafter.

Then, he said if there is indeed a Hereafter and a Last Day, he will find there better than what he has been given in the present life. As he thought that Allah the Almighty granted him all these blessings because He loves him and favors him to other people.

When his companion (the believing man) heard him saying so, he said to him, *(Do you disbelieve in Him Who created you out of dust (i.e. your father Adam), then out of Nutfah (mixed semen drops of male and female discharge), then fashioned you into a man?)* Do you disbelieve in the Day of Resurrection while you know that He, Allah, is Him Who created you out of dust, then out of Nutfah, then fashioned you in stages till you became a sound and well-erected man with hearing, sight, understanding and organs you transgress with! Then, how could you deny the Resurrection while you know that Allah is capable of creating you out of nothingness.

I do not worship other than Him and I believe in that He will resurrect the dead and gather the scattered and rotten bones together, and I know that there is no partner with Allah in His Dominion or creation, and that there is no god but Him.

Then, Allah the Almighty says: *(So his fruits were encircled (with ruin)),* i.e. all his fruits and plants were ruined and totally destroyed. *(And he remained clapping his hands (with sorrow) over what he had spent upon it, while it was all destroyed on its trellises)*

So, he regretted his previous acts and sayings that declared him as a disbeliever in Allah the Almighty and he could only say: *(Would that I had ascribed no partners to my Lord!)*. Then, Allah the Almighty says: And he had no group of men to help him against Allah, nor could he defend (or save) himself.

(He (Allah) is the Best for reward and the Best for the final end), i.e. trading with Allah is better than anything else as He gives the best of all rewards and with Him rests the best of all ends and goals.

Story Number 14:

People of the Garden

Surah al-Qalam 17-33

إِنَّا بَلَوْنَـٰهُمْ كَمَا بَلَوْنَآ أَصْحَـٰبَ ٱلْجَنَّةِ إِذْ أَقْسَمُوا۟ لَيَصْرِمُنَّهَا مُصْبِحِينَ ١٧

Indeed, We have tested those ˹Meccans˺ as We tested the owners of the garden—when they swore they would surely harvest ˹all˺ its fruit in the early morning,

وَلَا يَسْتَثْنُونَ ١٨

leaving no thought for Allah's Will.

فَطَافَ عَلَيْهَا طَآئِفٌ مِّن رَّبِّكَ وَهُمْ نَآئِمُونَ ١٩

Then it was struck by a torment from your Lord while they slept,

فَأَصْبَحَتْ كَٱلصَّرِيمِ ٢٠

so it was reduced to ashes.

It is a story about a group of people from the yemen. They were tested as the people of a garden containing different types of fruits and vegetation. They vowed between themselves during the night that they would pluck the fruit of the garden in the morning so that the poor and the beggars would not know what they were doing. In this way, they would be able to keep its fruits for themselves and not give any of it to charity, without saying "If Allah wills" therefore Allah *subhanahu wa ta'ala* broke their vow. They were so sure and confident of their power and authority that they swore they would surely pluck the fruit of their garden next morning, without feeling any need to say, "We shall do so if Allah so willed."

And so while they were asleep their garden was afflicted with a heavenly destruction from their Lord and it appeared as if it had been harvested, withered and dry. As the morning approached, they called each other to go together to pick the harvest or cut it. *"So they set out, while lowering their voices,"* (68: 23) meaning they spoke privately about what they were doing so that no one could hear what they said. Then Allah, the All-Knower of secrets and private discussions explained what they were saying in private.

They were telling each other to not allow any poor person to enter upon them in the garden today. They proceeded to their garden with strength and power thinking they had the power to do what they claimed and desired. But when they saw their garden withered and dry, they said, *"Indeed, we are lost,"* (68: 27). They thought they had lost their way and reached somewhere else because they remembered their garden being full of luster, brilliance and abundance of fruit. It was not black, gloomy and void of any benefit as what they saw before their eyes now. Then they changed their minds and realized with certainty that it was actually the correct path. Therefore, they said, *"Rather, we have been deprived,"* (68: 27) meaning nay, this is it, but we have no portion and no share of harvest.

"The awsat among them said, 'Did I not say to you: Why do you not exalt [Allah]?'" (68: 28). The *awsat* [أَوْسَطُهُمْ] among them means *'the most just of them and the best of them.'* Exalting Allah *subhanahu wa ta'ala* here means saying, "If Allah wills." That this *ayah* means that the best of them said to the others, "Did I not tell you, why don't you glorify Allah and thank Him for what He has given you and favored you with?"

They said, *"Exalted is our Lord! Indeed, we were wrongdoers,"* (68: 29), they became obedient when it was of no benefit to them, and they were remorseful and confessed when it was not of any use. Then they turned against one another blaming each other for what they had resolved to do, preventing the poor people from receiving their right of the harvest and fruit. Thus, their response to each other was only to confess their error and sin. This is the attitude of a person who is at fault, he blames other people for his mistakes. Allah *subhanahu wa ta'ala* has blessed each one of us with intellect. We are not making use of our brain and insight then we cannot blame others for our loss and failures.

They said, *"O woe to us; indeed we were transgressors,"* (68: 30), we have transgressed, trespassed, violated and exceeded the bounds until this happened to us. They repented to Allah *subhanahu wa ta'ala* and hoped for something better in exchange to their garden either in this life or in the abode of the Hereafter.

Allah *subhanahu wa ta'ala* ends the address by saying, *"Such is the punishment,"* (68: 33) of whoever opposes the command of Allah *subhanahu wa ta'ala,* is stingy with what Allah *subhanahu wa ta'ala* has given him and favored him with, withholds the right of the poor and needy, and responds to Allah's blessings upon him with ungratefulness (or disbelief). *"And the punishment of the Hereafter is greater, if they only knew,"* (68:33)

Story Number 15:

The Verse of Feeding

Sura al-Insān 7-9

يُوفُونَ بِٱلنَّذْرِ وَيَخَافُونَ يَوْمًا كَانَ شَرُّهُ مُسْتَطِيرًا ٧

وَيُطْعِمُونَ ٱلطَّعَامَ عَلَىٰ حُبِّهِ مِسْكِينًا وَيَتِيمًا وَأَسِيرًا ٨

إِنَّمَا نُطْعِمُكُمْ لِوَجْهِ ٱللَّهِ لَا نُرِيدُ مِنكُمْ جَزَآءً وَلَا شُكُورًا ٩

(These privileged servants of Allah are those) who fulfill their vows and keep fearing that Day whose severity spreads afar.And they give (their own) food, in deep love of Allah, to the needy, the orphan and prisoner (out of sacrifice, despite their own desire and need for it),(And say:) 'We are feeding you only to please Allah. We do not seek any recompense from you nor (wish for) any thanks. (Sura al-Ins n Verse 7-9)

Abdullah ibn Abbas(RA) narrates that once Imam Al-Hasan and Imam Al-Husayn R.A. fell ill and the Prophet SAW together with some of the companions , visited his sick grandsons. He SAW suggested that Sayyiduna Ali RA should make a vow to Allah for his sons' health. Heeding the Prophet's suggestion, Ali , Fatimah, along with their maid Fidda, took a vow that if the boys recovered, they would fast for three consecutive days.

Eventually they recovered and to fulfill the vow they also fasted along with their parents and maid. Since there was nothing in the house to eat, Sayyiduna Ali RA borrowed three measures of barley. Sayyidah Fatima RA ground one measure into flour and baked it into five loaves of bread equal to their number, and placed these before them for breaking the fast. Just then a beggar stopped at their door and said: *"Peace be upon you, O Ahlul Bayt of Muhammad! I am one of the poorest of Muslims , so can you please feed me and may Allah feed you the food of Paradise!"*

So they gladly gave him all the food they had and slept that night, tasting nothing but water.

They fasted again the next day and at sunset they placed the bread before them to break the fast, an orphan knocked on the door asking for food and they cheerfully fed him, themselves going without food for yet another day.

On the third day as the time to break their fast was approaching and the food was spread out before them, a prisoner of war suddenly appeared at their door and the same scenario was repeated, with the Prophet's Ahlul Bayt passing a third night without tasting a morsel of food.

When the dawn broke,Sayyiduna Ali RA, holding the hands of Sayyiduna Al-Hasan RA and Al-Husayn RA, came to the Prophet's house. The Prophet SAW seeing their pale countenances and noting they were trembling from hunger, expressed dismay and at once accompanied them to their house. On entering the house, he was shocked to see the sight of his daughter Sayyida Fatimah RA, sitting hollow eyed on her prayer mat, her stomach sunk into her back. It was, then, that the angel Jibreel came down with this verse, saying: "O Muhammad, Allah congratulates you for (the sacrifice) your household."

Then he recited the above-mentioned verse of feeding. This is how beautifully Allah rewarded the hunger and sacrifice of the household of the Prophet SAW.

Story Number 16:

Luqman the Wise Man

Surat al-Luqman 12, 13

وَلَقَدْ اٰتَيْنَا لُقْمٰنَ الْحِكْمَةَ اَنِ اشْكُرْ لِلّٰهِ وَمَنْ يَّشْكُرْ فَإِنَّمَا يَشْكُرُ لِنَفْسِهِ وَمَنْ كَفَرَ فَإِنَّ اللّٰهَ غَنِىٌّ حَمِيْدٌ ﴿٣١:١٢﴾

We bestow wisdom upon Luqman, (enjoining): "Give thanks to Allah." Whoso gives thanks to Allah, does so for his own good. And whoso disbelieves (let him know that) Allah is All-Sufficient, Immensely Praiseworthy.

وَاِذْ قَالَ لُقْمٰنُ لِا بْنِهٖ وَهُوَ يَعِظُهٗ يٰبُنَىَّ لَا تُشْرِكْ بِاللّٰهِ اِنَّ الشِّرْكَ لَظُلْمٌ عَظِيمٌ
۞٣١:١٣

And call to mind when Luqman said to his son while exhorting him: "My son, do not associate others with Allah in His Divinity.[20] Surely, associating others with Allah in His Divinity is a mighty wrong."

Luqman belonged to the black men of Egypt. He had thick lips and Allah the Almighty granted him wisdom but not prophethood. 'Umar Ibn Qais and Al-A'mash narrated: Luqman was a huge black slave, thick lipped. While he was preaching a man who used to know him saw him and said: **"Aren't you the slave of so and so who used to look after my sheep not so long in the past?"** Luqman said: **"Yes!"** The man said: **"What raised you to this high state I see?"**

Ibn Wahb narrates that Luqman's answer to the question about what had raised his status that people came to him for advice was: **"Lowering my gaze, watching my tongue, eating what is lawful, keeping my chastity, undertaking my promises, fulfilling my commitments, being hospitable to guests, respecting my neighbors, and discarding what does not concern me. All these made me the one you are looking at."** Abu Ad-Darda' added that Luqman the wise was granted wisdom because he was self-restrained, taciturn, deep-thinking, and he never slept during the day. No one had ever seen him observing trivialities, or foolishly laughing. He was very eloquent and well-versed. He did not weep or cry when all his children died. He even used to frequent the princes and men of authority to mediate. He was mentioned in the Glorious Qur'an and was highly praised by Allah the Almighty Who narrates his advice to his own son in which the first act that he forbids is *Shirk.*

The Prophet of Allah (S.A.W) also referred to Luqman's saying this to his son,

"O my son! Join not others in worship with Allah, verily joining others in worship with Allah is a great wrong indeed" (Luqman, 31:13).

The next advice that Luqman gives to his son and to mankind is taking care of parents. He states their rights over the children and tells the children to be kind to their parents even if they were polytheists. However, it is clarified that they should not be obeyed if they are inviting toward polytheism. This is followed by: *"O my son! If it be (anything) equal to the weight of a grain of mustard seed, and though it be in a rock, or in the heavens or in the earth, Allah will bring it forth. Verily, Allah is Subtle (in bringing out that grain), Well-Aware (of its place),"* i.e., he forbids wrong to the people even in the slightest way, for Allah will bring it forth and bring him to account on the Day of Resurrection.

Al- Khudri reported Prophet Muhammad (S.A.W) as saying: *"If any of you performs deeds in a solid rock that has no door or hole, his deeds, whatever they are, will come out (to the public)."*

Luqman's further advice to his son is: *"O my son! Aqim-As- Salah (perform As-Salah), enjoin (on people) Al-Ma'ruf (all that is good), and forbid (people) from Al-Munkar (i.e. disbelief in the Oneness of Allah, polytheists of all kinds and all that is evil and bad),* with your hand, with your tongue and if you could not, let it be with your heart.

Then, he advised him to observe patience, saying: *"and bear with patience whatever befalls you,"* because doing good and forbidding evil, will earn enmity from those who resent being corrected.

Luqman warns his son against the sin of pride: *"And turn not your face away from men with pride,"* cautioning against being showy or arrogant. Further, *"nor walk in insolence through the earth. Verily, Allah likes not any arrogant boaster."*

Luqman then advises his son to be moderate in his walking: *"And be moderate (or show no insolence) in your walking, and lower your voice,"* If you talk, do not raise your voice very loudly because the braying of the ass is the harshest of all voices.

Story number 17:

The Pit of Fire

Surah al-Buruj 1-10

قُتِلَ أَصْحَـٰبُ ٱلْأُخْدُودِ ٤

Condemned are the makers of the ditch—

ٱلنَّارِ ذَاتِ ٱلْوَقُودِ ٥

the fire ˹pit˺, filled with fuel—

إِذْ هُمْ عَلَيْهَا قُعُودٌ ٦

when they sat around it,

وَهُمْ عَلَىٰ مَا يَفْعَلُونَ بِٱلْمُؤْمِنِينَ شُهُودٌ ٧

watching what they had ˹ordered to be˺ done to the believers,

وَمَا نَقَمُوا۟ مِنْهُمْ إِلَّآ أَن يُؤْمِنُوا۟ بِٱللَّهِ ٱلْعَزِيزِ ٱلْحَمِيدِ ٨

who they resented for no reason other than belief in Allah—the Almighty, the Praiseworthy—

ٱلَّذِى لَهُۥ مُلْكُ ٱلسَّمَـٰوَٰتِ وَٱلْأَرْضِ ۚ وَٱللَّهُ عَلَىٰ كُلِّ شَىْءٍ شَهِيدٌ ٩

˹the One˺ to Whom belongs the kingdom of the heavens and earth. And Allah is a Witness over all things.

Around 70 years before the birth of Hazrat Muhammad SAW, there lived a king who had a sorcerer in his court. When he became old, he said to the king,

"I have become old and my time is nearly over, so send me a boy whom I can teach magic."

So, a young and intelligent boy was found as a student. The boy would go to the sorcerer everyday, but on his way he would see a monk. The monk used to sit alone, meditate, and worship Allah. He began to sit with the monk and listen to him.

He came toward the religion of truth, the religion of Allah. He had secretly come to the right path, but had to suffer a lot for that. The sorcerer would beat him for coming late, and then his father would beat him for reaching home late as well. But he persevered.

One day, he saw a huge animal on a bridge blocking the way for the people. The young boy picked a stone and said, if the God of the monk is the truth, then Oh Allah! Kill this animal with this stone.

The animal died. The people of the village said that the boy is blessed, and that he is gifted with sorcery. People used to bring their problems and ailments to this boy. He would pray to Allah, and Allah would fix all problems.

One day the wazir of the king's court came to the boy. He asked for a cure to his blindness. The boy said, ' I have nothing in my hands. All is the will of Allah Almighty. If you come to Allah, I may pray for you.'

The wazeer accepted Islam, and Allah gave him his eyesight back.

When the king got to know that the young boy named Abdullah, is spreading the message of Islam, he got furious. He was a yahoodi, who believed that Hazrat Isa A.S. was the dajjal, not a prophet. How could he tolerate, being a king, that his people believed in the prophethood of Hazrat Isa A.S. and the creator of Isa, the Almighty Allah.

The boy was summoned to court, and the king asked him to abandon his imaan. When the boy refused, he was taken to the top of a mountain to be killed. But by the grace and will of Allah almighty, a huge earthquake came and took away everyone on the mountain except for the boy.

He returned to the court alive and healthy.

The king again ordered his men to throw the boy in the water. Once again, a huge storm came and took away all the soldiers, leaving the boy safe and sound.

Brothers and sisters! Here comes the power of strong imaan.

The boy himself told the king how to kill him! He told him this secret but put one condition. The king accepted all terms. The boy said that I will tell you how to kill me, and you will kill me but your people will be there to witness it.

The king, as the boy told, shot an arrow at him by taking the name of Allah. And alas! The boy died.

Seeing all these miraculous incidents, twenty thousand poeple of that country accepted Islam.

The king who could not kill a single boy, now had to get rid of a whole nation of twenty thousand Muslims. He asked every one of them to abandon their faith, but nobody flinched. Such was the power of their imaan!

The king then dug a huge hole in the ground and arranged a huge fire in it. He then told every one of them to either leave their faith, or jump in the fire pit!

There was a woman among them, with a newborn baby. She thought for once to lie and save the life of the newborn.

But by the grace of Almighty, the baby spoke up and told his mother to choose the right path. And so she jumped in the burning fire pit along with her baby! In Surah al Buruj, Allah has pointed at the punishment that was then given to the makers of that fire ditch:

'The people of the pit were destroyed with fire abounding in fuel, while they sat around it, and were witnessing what they did to the believers.'

May Allah increase our imaan to heights of strength and glory.

Story Number 18:

Barsisa the Worshipper

(The Renegade)

Al-Hashr 16-17

كَمَثَلِ ٱلشَّيْطَـٰنِ إِذْ قَالَ لِلْإِنسَـٰنِ ٱكْفُرْ فَلَمَّا كَفَرَ قَالَ إِنِّى بَرِىٓءٌ مِّنكَ إِنِّىٓ أَخَافُ ٱللَّهَ رَبَّ ٱلْعَـٰلَمِينَ ١٦

˹They are˺ like Satan when he lures someone to disbelieve. Then after they have done so, he will say ˹on Judgment Day˺, "I have absolutely nothing to do with you. I truly fear Allah—the Lord of all worlds."

فَكَانَ عَـٰقِبَتَهُمَآ أَنَّهُمَا فِى ٱلنَّارِ خَـٰلِدَيْنِ فِيهَا ۚ وَذَٰلِكَ جَزَٰٓؤُا۟ ٱلظَّـٰلِمِينَ ١٧

So they will both end up in the Fire, staying there forever. That is the reward of the wrongdoers.

Once upon a time, there was a woman grazing sheep and goats. She had four brothers. They had to go out of town for some business, and they had to leave their sister behind. The people of the town suggested that they leave their sister with Barsisa, as he is the most pious man.

The monk, Barsisa, first refused, as he got scared of the responsibility. But he agreed, as the people of the town insisted for the security of the woman.

The monk committed adultery with her and she got pregnant. Satan came to him and said: Kill the woman and then bury her for you are a reputable and highly respected man (i.e. don't risk your own reputation for such a simple woman). The monk killed her and then buried her. Thereupon, Satan visited her four brothers in a dream while they were asleep and said to them: the monk committed adultery with your sister, and because she got pregnant, he killed her and buried her in such-and-such location. In the morning, one of them said: "By Allah! Last night I dreamt of something and I do not know whether to relate it to you or just keep it to myself?" They said: Relate it to us. He did so and one of them said: By Allah! I had the same dream.

Another said the same. And the fourth one said the same thing. They agreed that there must be something serious about that dream. They went to the king and appealed for his help against the monk. The king's troops came to arrest him and he was taken away. On the way, Satan came to the monk (and whispered in his ears): I set you up. No one else can save you from this. Prostrate yourself before me just for once and in return, I will save you from this. Thereupon, the monk prostrated himself before Satan. When they presented themselves before the king, Satan said to him: *I am free of you, I fear Allah, the Lord of the`Alamin (mankind, jinn and all that exists)!* "

Finally, the monk was killed.

Allah has narrated this incident to give this lesson: On the Day of Judgement, Satan himself will come forward and refuse to take all responsibility for misguiding man.

Story Number 19:

Repentance

27-28 Surah al-Anfaal

يَـٰٓأَيُّهَا ٱلَّذِينَ ءَامَنُوا۟ لَا تَخُونُوا۟ ٱللَّهَ وَٱلرَّسُولَ وَتَخُونُوٓا۟ أَمَـٰنَـٰتِكُمْ وَأَنتُمْ تَعْلَمُونَ ٢٧

O you who have believed, do not betray Allāh and the Messenger or betray your trusts while you know [the consequence].

وَٱعْلَمُوٓا۟ أَنَّمَآ أَمْوَٰلُكُمْ وَأَوْلَـٰدُكُمْ فِتْنَةٌ وَأَنَّ ٱللَّهَ عِندَهُۥٓ أَجْرٌ عَظِيمٌ ٢٨

And know that your wealth and your children are only a test and that with Allah is a great reward.

Ayats 27-28 of Surah Al-Anfal describe a story about Hazrat Abu Lubaba, one of the companions of Prophet Muhammad (SAW), during the Battle of Badr.

The Battle of Badr was a significant event in Islamic history and took place in the year 624 CE. The Muslims were greatly outnumbered, but they were able to emerge victorious with the help of Allah. During the battle, Hazrat Abu Lubaba was initially positioned with a group of Muslim fighters on a hill overlooking the battlefield. However, he became overcome with fear and began to doubt the outcome of the battle.

Feeling guilty for his momentary lapse in faith, Hazrat Abu Lubaba later approached Prophet Muhammad (SAW) and revealed his doubts. Seeking Allah's forgiveness, he tied himself to a pole in the mosque in Medina and vowed not to untie himself until Allah forgave him. The Prophet Muhammad (SAW) saw the sincerity of Hazrat Abu Lubaba's repentance and prayed for his forgiveness. Allah eventually forgave him, and he was released from his vow.

The story of Hazrat Abu Lubaba in Surah Al-Anfal emphasizes the importance of faith, sincerity, and repentance. It highlights the human nature of fear and doubt, but also emphasizes the importance of seeking forgiveness and turning back to Allah. The story of Hazrat Abu Lubaba serves as an example of how sincere repentance and seeking forgiveness can lead to redemption and salvation.

Story Number 20:

Owners of the Elephant

Surah al-fil 1-5

أَلَمْ تَرَ كَيْفَ فَعَلَ رَبُّكَ بِأَصْحَـٰبِ ٱلْفِيلِ ١

Have you not seen ˹O Prophet˺ how your Lord dealt with the Army of the Elephant?

أَلَمْ يَجْعَلْ كَيْدَهُمْ فِى تَضْلِيلٍ ٢

Did He not frustrate their scheme?

وَأَرْسَلَ عَلَيْهِمْ طَيْرًا أَبَابِيلَ ٣

For He sent against them flocks of birds,

تَرْمِيهِم بِحِجَارَةٍ مِّن سِجِّيلٍ ٤

that pelted them with stones of baked clay,

فَجَعَلَهُمْ كَعَصْفٍ مَّأْكُولٍ ٥

leaving them like chewed up straw.

The governor or viceroy, Abraha Al-Ashram built a huge and very lofty church, and wrote to the king of Abyssinia, Negus that "I have built you a church that is unprecedented, and I am intending to divert pilgrimage from Mecca to Abyssinia ",

Abraha Al-Ashram subjugated the Yemenites to build that church and forced them to taste several sorts of humiliation. He used to cut off the hand of the one who comes late for labor. He took many valuable things from the palace of Bilqis to add to the church. He took marbles, precious stones, and valuable luggage.

When the Arabs heard of the letter of Abraha sent to Negus, a man from Kinanah got angry. He set out till he reached the church where he urinated on its walls.

The news reached Abraha who asked about the doer. His men answered: this was done by one of those Arabs who perform pilgrimage to the Ka'bah at Mecca when he heard of your declared intention that you would divert pilgrimage from their Sacred House to your church.

Upon hearing this, Abraha burst with rage and took oath that he would demolish the Ka'bah. Then, he ordered the Abyssinians (Christians) to get prepared for war. He led a big expedition against Mecca accompanying elephants in his train.

Abraha sent Hanatah Al-Himiari to Mecca ordering him to ask about the chief of the people and tell him: "I (the king) did not come to fight against you, only came to destroy the Sacred House. If you do not stand in our way, we will not harm any of you all. 'Abraha added to his messenger: 'And if he showed his desire not to fight, bring him to me.'

When Hanatah entered Mecca, he asked about its chief and master. He was told: it is 'Abdul Muttalib Ibn Hashim. He saw him and thus delivered the message. 'Abdul Muttalib said: "By Allah! We do not intend to fight. Really we cannot afford it. This is the Sacred House of Allah and His Khalil (friend) Ibrahim (SAW), only Him Alone can protect it if He wills to." Upon hearing this, Hanatah said: "Come with me to meet with him (Abraha), he ordered me to do so." 'Abdul Muttalib set out for him accompanied by some of his sons till they approached the camp.

Abdul Muttalib entered the court of Abraha, as the chief of Quraysh.

Abraha said to his interpreter: Ask him what he wants?

Abraha was surprised to hear from 'Abdul Muttalib through the interpreter that all he wanted was compensation for his two hundred camels, but did not ask him to leave the Ka' bah alone. Actually, when Abraha entered the city of Makkah, he took away the camels of Abdul Muttalib.

When Abraha expressed surprise, 'Abdul Muttalib answered: "I am the master of the camels, whereas the Ka' bah house of worship -has its lord to defend it". Abraha said: No one can defend it from me. 'Abdul Muttalib said: You are on your own! Finally, Abraha gave him the camels back.

When 'Abdul Muttalib returned home he told the Quraishites about what happened between him and Abraha and ordered them to evacuate Mecca and move to the mountains.

In the morning, Abraha got prepared to enter Mecca, and got his elephant and troops prepared. The elephant's name was Mahmoud.

The elephant fell to the ground, when he was directed toward mecca.

The Abyssinians beat the elephant forcing him to stand up to his feet, but he refused. They hit his head with axe-like weapons, but he refused. They tried their best to force him to stand up to his feet, but they could not. They directed his face back towards Yemen and he stood up and ran towards it. They directed him towards the Sham (Syria) and then towards the east and he stood up to his feet and ran thereto. They again directed him towards Mecca, but he refused. Thereupon, Allah the Almighty sent upon them birds from the seaside resembling hawks. Each bird held three stones: one in his beak and two in his two legs. The stones were like chick-peas and lentils.

The Abyssinians fled away while death pursued them on every path and in every way and Abraha was hit with a stone as well. They carried him and his body began to tear up part after part till they reached Sanaa. After a short while, his chest cracked (as claimed by historians) and he died.

There are several lessons that can be learned from this beautiful story:

Envy is a disease, which only brings destruction. Abraha built a church in envy and also decided to attack the House of Allah. He himself was destroyed in the end.

Makkah is indeed a land blessed by Allah s.w.t ever since He first created heaven and earth. It is the land where Prophet Muhammad s.a.w was born, grew up and received the first revelation.

Dua and supplication are the most powerful weapons of a believer. Abdul Muttalib and his clan evacuated the place, but they also supplicated to Allah to protect the Kaaba.

Story Number 21:

Dhul Qarnayn

Surat al-Kahf 82-101

وَيَسْـَٔلُونَكَ عَن ذِى ٱلْقَرْنَيْنِ ۖ قُلْ سَأَتْلُواْ عَلَيْكُم مِّنْهُ ذِكْرًا ٨٣

They ask you ˹O Prophet˺ about Zul-Qarnain. Say, "I will relate to you something of his narrative."

إِنَّا مَكَّنَّا لَهُ فِى ٱلْأَرْضِ وَءَاتَيْنَـٰهُ مِن كُلِّ شَىْءٍ سَبَبًا ٨٤

Surely We established him in the land, and gave him the means to all things.

فَأَتْبَعَ سَبَبًا ٨٥ حَتَّىٰ إِذَا بَلَغَ مَغْرِبَ ٱلشَّمْسِ وَجَدَهَا تَغْرُبُ فِى عَيْنٍ حَمِئَةٍ وَوَجَدَ عِندَهَا قَوْمًا ۖ قُلْنَا يَـٰذَا ٱلْقَرْنَيْنِ إِمَّآ أَن تُعَذِّبَ وَإِمَّآ أَن تَتَّخِذَ فِيهِمْ حُسْنًا ٨٦

So he travelled a course, until he reached the setting ˹point˺ of the sun, which appeared to him to be setting in a spring of murky water, where he found some people. We said, "O Zul-Qarnain! Either punish them or treat them kindly."

Allah's Saying: *(And they ask you about Dhul--Qarnayn)* was revealed because the people of Quraish asked the Jews of something about which they would ask the Prophet Muhammad (SAW) to test his knowledge. The Jews told them: Ask him about a man who traveled through the earth, and about some young men who set out and no one knew what happened to them? Thereupon, Allah the Almighty revealed the stories of the Owners of the Cave and that of Dhul-Qarnayn. Thus, He said: *(Say: I shall recite to you something of his story)*, i.e. enough and sufficient news about him and his status. Then, He said: *(Verily, We established him in the earth, and We gave him the means of everything)*, i.e. Allah the Almighty expanded his kingdom and provided him with what might enable him to gain what he wished to. Narrated Qutaibah that 'Ali Ibn Abu Talib was once asked about Dhul-Qarnayn: how could he reach the east and west? 'Ali replied: The clouds were subjugated for him, the means (of everything) were provided to him.'Ali added: Do you want me to go on? The man became silent and thereupon, 'Ali R.A. became silent.

Dhul-Qarnayn performed the Pilgrimage on foot. Upon hearing that, Ibrahim (SAW) met him and in their meeting he invoked Allah for his sake, and advised him. It was said also that he was brought a horse to ride, but he said: I do not ride (on the back of horses) in a land wherein Prophet Ibrahim (SAW). Hence, Allah the Almighty subjugated for him the clouds, and Ibrahim (SAW) gave him the glad tidings pertaining to this. The clouds used to carry him anywhere he wished for.

Dhul-Qarnayn was known for traveling to the three corners of the world. He spent thousands of years traveling, spreading the name and message of Allah. On one of his journeys, he reached the place that no one can ever overpass, and he stood on the edge of the western ocean called Oqyanus wherein the islands called *Al-Khalidat* "The Eternal Ones". There, he could watch the setting of the sun.There was a lake with dark, thick waters. This was the west of the world.

About the people of that region, the ayat of the Quran says, *(We (Allah) said (by inspiration): "O Dhul Qarnain! Either you punish them, or treat them with kindness.")*

Dhul-Qarnayn chooses to punish those who do wrong, and also warns them of the punishment in the hereafter.

He shows kindness to those who believe in Allah's Oneness and work righteousness, and spoke to them about the rewards in the Hereafter.

Without a shadow of doubt, those who do wrong will be punished by Allah with a terrible torment, while those who believe and do good deeds will be rewarded with paradise.

Then he set out on another journey and reached the end of the eastern world. This was the end of the civilized people. Beyond this was the territory of barbaric people. They killed people from other tribes, they had a strange language, and they could not understand anything.

Allah the Almighty says: *(then, he followed (another) way. Until, when he reached between two mountains, he found, before (near) them (those two mountains), a people who scarcely understood a word)*

People from the nearby towns told him that Gog and Magog wronged them and practiced mischief in their land. They offered him a tribute for that he builds a barrier (dam) preventing them from raiding over them. He refused to take the tribute they offered him, finding sufficiency in that which Allah the Almighty has given him, so *(He said: "That (wealth, authority and power) in which my Lord had established me is better (than your tribute)).* Then, he asked them to bring him men and tools to erect the barrier between them. Gog and Magog could only reach them from that place located between two mountain-cliffs. The other paths were either vast seas, or high mountains. Consequently, he erected it using iron and molten copper: he put iron instead of bricks and molten copper instead of clay. Allah the Almighty commented, *(So they (Gog and Magog) could not scale it)* with escalators, *(or dig through it)* with axes or picks. *((Dhul-Qarnayn) said: "This is a mercy from my Lord)* i.e. Allah the Almighty decreed this to be a mercy from Him to His slaves that they no longer be assaulted by Gog and Magog.

The lesson in this verse for us laymen is, to use the means that Allah has given to us, to spread good to others who dwell beyond our own comfortable little circles. We live in an era in which we can do much to benefit others across the globe, because many people now have a screen on their palms, laps, desks or tablets through which they can read our writing and hear our voices within seconds.

Story Number 22

Ghazwa e Badr

Ayats 29-30 Surah al Anfal

يَـٰٓأَيُّهَا ٱلَّذِينَ ءَامَنُوٓا۟ إِن تَتَّقُوا۟ ٱللَّهَ يَجْعَل لَّكُمْ فُرْقَانًا وَيُكَفِّرْ عَنكُمْ سَيِّـَٔاتِكُمْ وَيَغْفِرْ لَكُمْ وَٱللَّهُ ذُو ٱلْفَضْلِ ٱلْعَظِيمِ ٢٩

O believers! If you are mindful of Allah, He will grant you a standard ˹to distinguish between right and wrong˺, absolve you of your sins, and forgive you. And Allah is the Lord of infinite bounty.

وَإِذْ يَمْكُرُ بِكَ ٱلَّذِينَ كَفَرُوا۟ لِيُثْبِتُوكَ أَوْ يَقْتُلُوكَ أَوْ يُخْرِجُوكَ وَيَمْكُرُونَ وَيَمْكُرُ ٱللَّهُ وَٱللَّهُ خَيْرُ ٱلْمَـٰكِرِينَ ٣٠

And ˹remember, O Prophet,˺ when the disbelievers conspired to capture, kill, or exile you. They planned, but Allah also planned. And Allah is the best of planners.

The verses detail the plans of the non-believers of Makkah to attack the Muslims and how Allah protected the Muslims from their evil intentions.

The non-believers, led by Abu Jahl, had prepared a well-equipped army to confront the Muslims. When they learned that the Muslims were also preparing for battle, they decided to send spies to gather information about the Muslim army. The spies returned with news that the Muslims were poorly equipped and low in number, which gave the non-believers a false sense of confidence.

Allah also reveals to His Prophet Muhammad SAW that the non-believers are planning to deal with you in one of the three ways: kill you, kidnap you, or exile you. When Abu Talib asked his nephew, *'Do you know what conspiracies the non-believers have been planning against you?'*

Prophet Muhammad SAW answered, *'Without doubt, my Protector, my Creator has not kept me ignorant. I know.'*

Allah had different plans. And His plans were superior to those of the non-believers. He sent angels to assist the Muslim army and protect them from the non-believers.

The non-believers' plans were no match for Allah's divine plan. Despite their well-equipped army and their attempts to gather intelligence on the Muslim army, Allah was able to protect the Muslims and give them victory in the battle.

The incident described in these verses serves as a reminder of the power of Allah and the importance of relying on Him in times of difficulty and hardship.

It also emphasizes the importance of having faith and trust in Allah's divine plan, even in the face of seemingly insurmountable obstacles. Overall, the verses in Surah Al-Anfal provide a message of hope and encouragement for Muslims, reminding them that Allah is always with them and will protect them from the schemes of their enemies.

Story Number 23:

Asiya, the Foster Mother of Musa

Surah al-Qasas 7-9

وَأَوْحَيْنَاۤ إِلَىٰٓ أُمِّ مُوسَىٰٓ أَنْ أَرْضِعِيهِ ۖ فَإِذَا خِفْتِ عَلَيْهِ فَأَلْقِيهِ فِى ٱلْيَمِّ وَلَا تَخَافِى وَلَا تَحْزَنِىٓ ۖ إِنَّا رَادُّوهُ إِلَيْكِ وَجَاعِلُوهُ مِنَ ٱلْمُرْسَلِينَ ٧

We inspired the mother of Musa: "Nurse him, but when you fear for him, put him then into the river, and do not fear or grieve. We will certainly return him to you, and make him one of the messengers."

فَٱلْتَقَطَهُۥٓ ءَالُ فِرْعَوْنَ لِيَكُونَ لَهُمْ عَدُوًّا وَحَزَنًا ۗ إِنَّ فِرْعَوْنَ وَهَـٰمَـٰنَ وَجُنُودَهُمَا كَانُوا۟ خَـٰطِـِٔينَ ٨

And ʿit so happened thatʾ Firoun's people picked him up, only to become their enemy and source of grief. Surely Firoun, Hamân, and their soldiers were sinful.

وَقَالَتِ ٱمْرَأَتُ فِرْعَوْنَ قُرَّتُ عَيْنٍ لِّى وَلَكَ ۖ لَا تَقْتُلُوهُ عَسَىٰ أَن يَنفَعَنَا أَوْ نَتَّخِذَهُ وَلَدًا وَهُمْ لَا يَشْعُرُونَ ٩

Firoun's wife said ʿto himʾ, "ʿThis baby isʾ a source of joy for me and you. Do not kill him. Perhaps he may be useful to us or we may adopt him as a son." They were unaware ʿof what was to comeʾ.

Asiya, the wife of Firoun, was no ordinary woman. Her strength and her status will forever remain unsurpassed.

She was a woman who never allowed herself to be defined or limited by her painful circumstances, but rather carried in her such a deep faith and sense of self that she was willing to die for what she believed in.

It was for this reason that Prophet Muhammad (SAW) mentioned her as one of the greatest women of all time.

One day, Prophet Muhammad said:

"Many men reached perfection but none among the women reached perfection except Mary, the daughter of ʿ`Imran, and Asya, Firoun's wife. And the superiority of `Aisha to other women is like the superiority of Tharid to other kinds of food." (Al-Bukhari)

Asiya's story begins in Egypt where she lived with her husband, Firoun — known as the greatest tyrant of all time. After being told by a fortune teller that he would be overtaken by a man from the Children of Israel, Firoun ordered all male babies to be executed.

The Noble Quran describes the horrific life of the Children of Israel as follows:

(And remember, We delivered you from the people of Firoun: They set you hard tasks and punishments, slaughtered your sons and let your women live; therein was a tremendous trial from your Lord.) (2:49)

So when Prophet Musa (SAW) was born, his mother feared for his life. But Allah assured her that he would be safe, and told her to place him in a basket and put him on the Nile.

And just as Allah had promised, Prophet Musa came safely to shore, where he was found by Asiya, who was able to convince her husband to keep the child. Allah says in the Quran what means:

(Then the household of Firoun picked him up, that he might become for them an enemy and a (cause of) grief. Verily! Firoun, Haman and their hosts were sinners. And the wife of Firoun said: "A comfort of the eye for me and for you. Kill him not, perhaps he may be of benefit to us, or we may adopt him as a son." And they perceive not (the result of that).)

So Musa grew, under the protection of Asiya, in the house of Firoun. Musa grew to be a great prophet, who called his people to the worship of the one Allah. But because of the oppression of Firoun, few people believed in him.

Firoun proclaimed himself as Allah, and many of the Children of Israel were terrified to disobey him. Allah says in the Quran what means:

(Then he collected (his men) and made a proclamation, saying, "I am your Lord, Most High.") (79: 23-4)

For those who had dared disobey Firoun and believe in Musa, was a grave punishment. When the magicians realized the truth of Musa' message, they immediately believed in the one true Allah.

To them Firoun said:

(Believe ye in Him before I give you permission? Surely this must be your leader, who has taught you magic! Be sure I will cut off your hands and feet on opposite sides, and I will have you crucified on trunks of palm-trees: so shall ye know for certain, which of us can give the more severe and the more lasting punishment!) (20:71)

Yet despite this persecution, Asiya believed in Musa' message and held firmly to her faith. That faith was so strong, she was willing to die for it. When Firoun found out what she believed, he tortured her severely.

Her belief in Allah was so strong, it made her an ever-lasting symbol:

{Allah sets forth an example for those who believe — the wife of Firoun who said: "My Lord, build for me with Thee a house in heaven, and save me from the Firoun and his doings, and save me from an unjust people."} (66:11)

Asiya was a queen. She was the wife of one of the most powerful men to walk the earth. She lived a life of unparalleled wealth and luxury. And yet, she knew that her true home was in Paradise.

She had no attachment to this life. Asiya was not defined by the wickedness of the man she married. Her mind and her soul remained independent from her husband. And her heart was not a slave to his beliefs. She refused to submit to the tyranny of her husband, but chose instead to devout her soul and her life to Allah.

And in the story of Asiya is an everlasting example of a woman who chose the Hereafter over all of the glitter of this world, and whose love for Allah and the Home with Him inspired her to take on the greatest tyrant of all time and give her life in the process.

Story Number 24:

The Morning Sunlight

Surah al Dhuhaa 1-8

وَٱلضُّحَىٰ ١وَٱلَّيْلِ إِذَا سَجَىٰ ٢

By the morning sunlight, and the night when it falls still!

مَا وَدَّعَكَ رَبُّكَ وَمَا قَلَىٰ ٣ وَلَلْءَاخِرَةُ خَيْرٌ لَّكَ مِنَ ٱلْأُولَىٰ ٤

Your Lord ˹O Prophet˺ has not abandoned you, nor has He become hateful ˹of you˺. And the next life is certainly far better for you than this one.

وَلَسَوْفَ يُعْطِيكَ رَبُّكَ فَتَرْضَىٰ ٥أَلَمْ يَجِدْكَ يَتِيمًا فَـَٔاوَىٰ ٦

And ˹surely˺ your Lord will give so much to you that you will be pleased. Did He not find you as an orphan then sheltered you?

وَوَجَدَكَ ضَآلًّا فَهَدَىٰ ٧ وَوَجَدَكَ عَآئِلًا فَأَغْنَىٰ ٨

Did He not find you unguided then guided you? And did He not find you needy then satisfied your needs?

After a long and continuous while of revelations, Allah stopped sending the verses of the Quran. There was absolutely no communication, no message from the heavens. Prophet Muhammad SAW began to doubt himself, whether he had made some mistake that Allah had stopped talking to His beloved.

He SAW was feeling depressed and hopeless. He was worried that if the revelation would not come, people would further ridicule his mission and message of Allah.

One day, when Prophet SAW was in his hujra, Hazrat Khadija gently asked, 'Is Allah angry with you?'

Muhammad SAW was already devastated; upon hearing this, tears appeared in his eyes.

Immediately, Hazrat Jibrael A.S. came with the most beautiful words of revelation.

The Prophet is reassured, by the Master of the Heavens and the Earth: *"Your Rabb has not at all forsaken you, nor is he displeased with you."* Then, he is given the good news that the hardships that he was experiencing in the initial stage of his mission will not last long and the later period of life for him will be better than the former period. Before long, Allah will bless him so abundantly that he will be well pleased. This is one of the express prophecies of the Qur'an, which proved literally true later on. When this prophecy was made, there seemed not to be the remotest chance that the helpless and powerless man who had come out to wage a war against ignorance and paganism would ever achieve such wonderful success.

The Prophet (SAW) is then told: "What made you think that your Rabb has forsaken you, and that We are displeased with you? Whereas the fact is that We have been good to you with kindness after kindness ever since the day of your birth. You were born an orphan, We made the best arrangement for your upbringing and care: you were unaware of the Way, We showed you the Way; you were indigent, We made you rich. All this shows that you have been favored by Us from the very beginning and Our grace and bounty has been constantly focussed on you." These are the similar words which Allah said to console Prophet Musa when he was sent to Pharaoh as described in Surah TuaHa: *"We have been looking after you with kindness ever since your birth; therefore, you should be satisfied that you will not be left alone in this dreadful mission. Our bounty will constantly be with you." (37-42)*

One of the key lessons that we can learn from Surah Ad-Dhuha is that even in the midst of darkness and difficulties, there is always hope for a brighter tomorrow. The Surah speaks about the Prophet's difficult times, and reassures him that Allah has not abandoned him, and that there is a great reward waiting for him in the Hereafter.

Another lesson we can learn from Surah Ad-Dhuha is the importance of gratitude. The Surah encourages the Prophet Muhammad (peace be upon him) to be grateful for the blessings that he has received from Allah, and to remember that Allah has always been there for him, even when he may have felt alone or abandoned.

Stories 25:

Hazrat Yusuf A.S.

Surah al-Yusuf 1-111

لَّقَدْ كَانَ فِى يُوسُفَ وَإِخْوَتِهِ ءَايَـٰتٌ لِّلسَّآئِلِينَ ٧

Indeed, in the story of Yusuf A.S. and his brothers there are lessons for all who ask.

إِذْ قَالُواْ لَيُوسُفُ وَأَخُوهُ أَحَبُّ إِلَىٰ أَبِينَا مِنَّا وَنَحْنُ عُصْبَةٌ إِنَّ أَبَانَا لَفِى ضَلَـٰلٍ مُّبِينٍ ٨

˹Remember˺ when they said ˹to one another˺, "Surely Yusuf A.S. and his brother ˹Benjamin˺ are more beloved to our father than we, even though we are a group of so many.1 Indeed, our father is clearly mistaken.

ٱقْتُلُواْ يُوسُفَ أَوِ ٱطْرَحُوهُ أَرْضًا يَخْلُ لَكُمْ وَجْهُ أَبِيكُمْ وَتَكُونُواْ مِنْ بَعْدِهِ قَوْمًا صَـٰلِحِينَ ٩

Kill Yusuf A.S. or cast him out to some ˹distant˺ land so that our father's attention will be only ours, then after that you may ˹repent and˺ become righteous people!"

قَالَ قَآئِلٌ مِّنْهُمْ لَا تَقْتُلُواْ يُوسُفَ وَأَلْقُوهُ فِى غَيَـٰبَتِ ٱلْجُبِّ يَلْتَقِطْهُ بَعْضُ ٱلسَّيَّارَةِ إِن كُنتُمْ فَـٰعِلِينَ ١٠

One of them said, "Do not kill Yusuf A.S.. But if you must do something, throw him into the bottom of a well so perhaps he may be picked up by some travelers."

As the sun appeared over the horizon, bathing the earth in its morning glory, Yusuf A.S., son of the Prophet Yaqub A.S. awoke from his sleep, delighted by a pleasant dream he had had. Filled with excitement he ran to his father and related it.

"O my father! Verily, I saw (in a dream) eleven stars and the sun and the moon, I saw them prostrating themselves to me." (Ch 12:4)

His father's face lit up. He foresaw that Yusuf A.S. would be one through whom the prophecy of his grandfather, Prophet Ibrahim A.S., would be fulfilled.

However, the father was well aware of the jealousy of Yusuf A.S.'s brothers, so he warned him against telling his dream to his brothers.

Yusuf A.S. was eighteen years old, very handsome and robust, with a gentle temperament. His brother Benjamin was equally pleasant. Both were from one mother, Rachel. Because of their refined qualities, the father loved the two more than his other children, and would not let them out of his sight.

Yusuf's brothers plotted against him. One of them said: *"Kill not Yusuf A.S., but if you must do something, throw him down to the bottom of a well, he will be picked up by some caravan of travelers."*

They said: "O our father! Why do you not trust us with Yusuf, when we are indeed his well wishers? Send him with us tomorrow to enjoy himself and play, and we will take care of him."

Yaqub A.S. said: "Truly, it saddens me that you should take him away. I fear lest a wolf should devour him, while you are careless of him."

They said: "If a wolf devours him, while we are Usbah (a strong group) (to guard him), then surely we are the losers."

On leaving home, they went directly to the well, as they had planned. One of them put his arms around Yusuf A.S. and held him tightly. Startled by this unusual behavior, Yusuf A.S. struggled to free himself. More brothers rushed to hold him. One of them removed his shirt. Some more joined in to lift Yusuf A.S. up and cast him into the deep well. Yusuf A.S.'s piteous pleas made no difference to their cruel hearts.

There was water in the well, which buoyed Yusuf A.S.'s body, so he was not harmed.

Then they killed a sheep and soaked Yusuf A.S.'s shirt in its blood. *'And they came to their father in the early part of the night weeping.'(Ch 12:16)*

They told their father crying, *'O our father! We went racing with one another, and left Yusuf A.S. with our belongings and a wolf devoured him; but you will never believe us even when we speak the truth.' (Ch 12:17)*

He held the blood stained in his hands, spread it out and remarked: *"What a merciful wolf! He ate up my beloved son without tearing his shirt!"* Their faces turned red when he demanded more information, but each swore by Allah that he was telling the truth. The broken-hearted father burst into tears: *"Nay! But your own selves have made up a tale. So for me patience is more fitting. It is Allah Alone whose Help can be sought against that which you assert." (Ch 12:18)*

The caravan of merchants halted at this famous well for water. A man lowered in his bucket. Yusuf A.S. was startled by the bucket hurtling down and grabbed hold of it. He took out the bucket, and was left amazed!

Standing before them was a healthy, handsome youth, beaming with an angelic smile. Immediately, they clapped iron shackles on his feet and took him along to Egypt.

They sold him for a low price, for a few Dirhams. Aziz, the chief minister from Egypt took him home.

Yusuf A.S. felt at ease, for at last he was sheltered and would be well cared for. He thanked Allah over and over and wondered at the mystery of life.

Yusuf A.S.'s handsomeness became the talk of the town. People referred to him as the most attractive man they had ever seen and wrote poetry about him. His face carried immaculate beauty. The purity of his inner soul and his heart showed in his face, increasing his beauty. People from afar came to the city to have a glimpse of him.

The wife of the chief minister, Zulaikha, watched Yusuf A.S. from day to day. She ate with him, talked with him, listened to him, and her wonder increased over the passion of time.

The chief minister's wife, Zulaikha could not resist the handsome Yusuf A.S., and her obsession with him caused her sleepless nights. She fell in love with him.

Allah the Almighty told us: '*And she, in whose house he was, sought to seduce him (to do an evil act), she closed the doors and said: "come on, O you." He said: "I seek refuge in Allah! Truly he (your husband) is my master! He made my stay agreeable! (So I will never betray him). Verily, the Zalimun (wrong, evildoers) will never be successful."*

Yusuf A.S.'s refusal only heightened her passion. As he moved to the door to escape, she ran after him and caught hold of his shirt. In her tugging she tore his shirt and held the torn piece in her hand. They reached the door together. It opened suddenly, there stood her husband and a relative of hers.

The sly woman immediately changed her tone to anger, and, showing the torn piece of the shirt in her hand, asked her husband: "*What is the recompense (punishment) for him who intended an evil design against your wife, except that he be put in prison or a painful torment?"* (Ch 12:25)

The shirt was passed from hand to hand, while she watched. The witness (her cousin) looked at it and found that it was torn at the back. The evidence showed that she was guilty. The disappointed husband remarked to his wife: *"Surely, it is a plot of you women! Certainly mighty is your plot!" (Ch 12:28)*

An incident like this cannot remain a secret in a house filled with servants, and the story spread. Women began to see her behavior as scandalous.

Zuleikha honestly believed that it was not easy for any woman to resist a man as handsome as Yusuf A.S.. To prove her helplessness, she planned to subject the women to the same temptation she faced. She invited them to a lavish banquet.

After finishing their dinner, the guests began cutting their fruit. At that very moment she summoned Yusuf A.S. to make his appearance. Zulaikha called him by his name and he raised his head. The guests were astonished and dumbfounded. His face was shining and full of an angelic beauty.

They exclaimed in astonishment while continuing to cut the fruit. All their eyes were on Yusuf A.S. So it was that the women began to cut their palms absent-mindedly without feeling that they had cut them.

That evening, Zulaikha convinced her husband that the only way to save her honor was to put Yusuf A.S. in prison; otherwise she would not be able to control herself or to safeguard his prestige.

Prison was Yusuf's A.S. third test. During this period Allah blessed him with an extraordinary gift; the ability to interpret dreams.

At about the same time two other men landed in the prison. One was the cupbearer of the king; the other was the king's cook.

The king's cook dreamed that he stood in a place with bread on his head, and two birds were eating the bread. The cupbearer dreamed that he was serving the king wine. The two went to Yusuf A.S. and told him their dreams, asking him to give them their meaning.

First, Yusuf A.S. called them to Allah. Then he said that the cook would be crucified until he died and that the cupbearer would return to the service of the king. Yusuf A.S. told the cupbearer to remember him to the king and to say that there was a wronged soul called Yusuf A.S. in prison. What Yusuf A.S. predicted did happen; the cook was crucified and the cupbearer returned to the palace.

After the cupbearer returned to service, Satan made him forget to mention Yusuf A.S.'s name to the king. Therefore, Yusuf A.S. remained in prison for a few years, but he made patience his own, praying to Allah.

One night, the king had a dream. He sees himself on the banks of the Nile river. The water is receding before him, becoming mere mud. The fish begin to skip and jump in the mud. Seven fat cows come out of the river followed by seven lean cows. The seven lean ones devour the seven fat ones. The king is terrified. The seven ears of green grain grow on the riverbanks and disappear in the mud. One the same spot grows seven dray ears of grain.

Upon hearing this, the cupbearer remembered the dream interpreter, Yusuf he had met in prison. The king sent him to Yusuf, for the interpretation of the dream.

Yusuf A.S. interpreted it to him: "There will be seven years of abundance. If the land is properly cultivated, there will be an excess of good harvest, more than the people will need. This should be stored. Thereafter, seven years of famine will follow, during which time the excess grain could be used."

"After seven years of drought, there will be a year during which water will be plentiful. If the water is properly used, grapevines and olive trees will grow in abundance, providing plenty of grapes and olive oil."

The cupbearer hurried back with the good news. The king was fascinated by Yusuf A.S.'s interpretation.

He commanded his men that Yusuf A.S. be set free from prison and presented to him at once. Yusuf A.S. refused to leave the prison unless his innocence was proven.

The king ordered: *"Bring the wives of the ministers and the wife of the chief minister at once."*

The eyes of everyone turned to the wife of the chief minister. She boldly confessed that she had lied: "I tempted him; but he refused."

The king informed Yusuf A.S. that his innocence was established and ordered him to come to the palace to meet him. The king recognized his noble qualities.

The king offered him a high position. During the seven good years, Yusuf A.S. had full control over the cultivation and storage of crops. During the following seven years, drought followed and famine spread throughout the region, including Canaan, the homeland of Yusuf A.S.

Yaqub A.S. sent ten of his sons, all except Benjamin, to Egypt to purchase provisions. Yusuf A.S. heard of the ten brothers who had come from afar and who could not speak the language of the Egyptians. When they called on him to purchase their needs, Yusuf A.S. immediately recognized his brothers, but they did not know him.

The brothers returned to their father. They told their father to send Benjamin with them the next time, otherwise, they won't give us supplies.

Yaqub A.S. became sad and told them: "I will not send him with you unless you give me a pledge in Allah's name that you shall bring him back to me as safely as you take him." They gave their solemn pledge.

Yusuf A.S. welcomed them heartily. He prepared a feast for them and seated them in pairs. Yusuf A.S. arranged to sit next to his beloved brother Benjamin.

That night, when Yusuf A.S. and Benjamin were alone in a room, he said:

'My loving brother, I am the brother who was lost and whose name you are constantly repeating. Fate has brought us together after many years of separation. This is Allah's favor. But let it be a secret between us for the time being.'

The next day, while their bags were being filled with grains to load onto the camels, Yusuf A.S. ordered one of his attendants to place the king's gold cup into Benjamin's saddlebag. When the brothers were ready to set out, the gates were locked, and the court crier shouted: "O you travelers, you are thieves!"

Benjamin was kept behind as a punishment for theft. The brothers reluctantly left for their home, and told their father that Benjamin had been involved in theft.

Yaqub A.S. again opted for patience. After a few years, they again went to Egypt for food and grains. They begged Yusuf A.S. And in response, Yusuf A.S. told them that I am the brother that you had thrown in the well. Benjamin, here is my brother. Go bring my father.

Yusuf A.S. forgives his brothers, and the sight of his father also returns. The meeting of the father and the son after years of trials and tribulations was intense and heart-touching.

The story of Yusuf teaches us precious lessons of the importance of patience and keeping strong faith in Almighty Allah.

Story Number 26:

When the Earth is Shaken

Surah Al-Zalzalah, 99:1-5

إِذَا زُلْزِلَتِ ٱلْأَرْضُ زِلْزَالَهَا ١ وَأَخْرَجَتِ ٱلْأَرْضُ أَثْقَالَهَا ٢

When the earth is shaken in its ultimate quaking, and when the earth throws out all its contents,

وَقَالَ ٱلْإِنسَٰنُ مَا لَهَا ٣ يَوْمَئِذٍ تُحَدِّثُ أَخْبَارَهَا ٤ بِأَنَّ رَبَّكَ أَوْحَىٰ لَهَا ٥

and humanity cries, "What is wrong with it?"– on that Day the earth will recount everything, having been inspired by your Lord ˹to do so˺.

There is a tradition which says that once a man came to the holy Prophet (SAW) and asked him to teach him something from what Allah had taught him. The holy Prophet (SAW) sent him to one of his followers to teach him the Quran. He taught the man Surah Zalzalah to the end. Then, the man was ready to leave saying that that was sufficient for him.

Here is how Quran describes the Day of Judgement:

"But when there comes the Deafening Blast On the Day a man will flee from his brother And his mother and his father And his wife and his children, For every man, that Day, will be a matter adequate for him.[Some] faces, that Day, will be bright -Laughing, rejoicing at good news. And [other] faces, that Day, will have upon them dust. Blackness will cover them. Those are the disbelievers, the wicked ones." (Quran 80:33-42).

Those who will be alive when the Trumpet is blown will taste death and the dead will come to life. Each man will be answerable for his own deeds and will have no one to share the burden of his deeds – may they be good or bad. For those who doubt the procession of these events, Allah clarifies in the Quran saying:

"O People, if you should be in doubt about the Resurrection, then [consider that] indeed, We created you from dust, then from a sperm-drop, then from a clinging clot, and then from a lump of flesh, formed and unformed - that We may show you. And We settle in the wombs whom We will for a specified term, then We bring you out as a child, and then [We develop you] that you may reach your

[time of] maturity. And among you is he who is taken in [early] death, and among you is he who is returned to the most decrepit [old] age so that he knows, after [once having] knowledge, nothing. And you see the earth barren, but when We send down upon it rain, it quivers and swells and grows [something] of every beautiful kind. That is because Allah is the Truth and because He gives life to the dead and because He is over all things competent And [that they may know] that the Hour is coming - no doubt about it - and that Allah will resurrect those in the graves" (Quran 22:5-7).

The Resurrection of the dead and the death of all men is the Promise of our Lord and certainly, He does not go against what He promises.

Abu Huraira reported that the Messenger of Allah (SAW) said:

"The people will be gathered on the Day of Resurrection on reddish white land like a pure loaf (of bread). That land will have no landmarks for anyone (to recognize it). They will not be having any provisions with them. They will be given to drink out of a single water-course which will have mire in it, and their drink will be like syrup in thickness. Their food will be the fruit of different kinds of thorny trees which will neither fatten nor satisfy hunger. Then they will come to the Sirat (the bridge over Hell). The first to pass over it would be like a flash of lightning, the second like the wink of an eye, and the third (like a wind which would be)

driven (towards Paradise) and there would be none among them who would not be given the task of crossing it (i.e. Hell) and this is (the meaning) of Allah's Statement, "We shall rescue those who kept from evil and We shall leave the wrong-doers therein to their knees." (Quran, 19:72)"

When Ibrahim built the House of Allah with His Son

Surah al-baqarah 125-129

وَإِذْ جَعَلْنَا ٱلْبَيْتَ مَثَابَةً لِّلنَّاسِ وَأَمْنًا وَٱتَّخِذُوا مِن مَّقَامِ إِبْرَٰهِـمَ مُصَلًّى ۖ وَعَهِدْنَآ إِلَىٰٓ إِبْرَٰهِـمَ وَإِسْمَـٰعِيلَ أَن طَهِّرَا بَيْتِىَ لِلطَّآئِفِينَ وَٱلْعَـٰكِفِينَ وَٱلرُّكَّعِ ٱلسُّجُودِ ١٢٥

And ˹remember˺ when We made the Sacred House a center and a sanctuary for the people ˹saying˺, "˹You may˺ take the standing-place of Ibrahim as a site of prayer." And We entrusted Ibrahim and Ismail to purify My House for those who circle it, who meditate in it, and who bow and prostrate themselves ˹in prayer˺.

وَإِذْ قَالَ إِبْرَٰهِـمُ رَبِّ ٱجْعَلْ هَـٰذَا بَلَدًا ءَامِنًا وَٱرْزُقْ أَهْلَهُ مِنَ ٱلثَّمَرَٰتِ مَنْ ءَامَنَ مِنْهُم بِٱللَّهِ وَٱلْيَوْمِ ٱلْءَاخِرِ ۖ قَالَ وَمَن كَفَرَ فَأُمَتِّعُهُ قَلِيلًا ثُمَّ أَضْطَرُّهُ إِلَىٰ عَذَابِ ٱلنَّارِ ۖ وَبِئْسَ ٱلْمَصِيرُ ١٢٦

And ´remember˥ when Ibrahim said, "My Lord, make this city ´of Mecca˥ secure and provide fruits to its people—those among them who believe in Allah and the Last Day." He answered, "As for those who disbelieve, I will let them enjoy themselves for a little while, then I will condemn them to the torment of the Fire. What an evil destination!"

وَإِذْ يَرْفَعُ إِبْرَٰهِـۧمُ ٱلْقَوَاعِدَ مِنَ ٱلْبَيْتِ وَإِسْمَٰعِيلُ رَبَّنَا تَقَبَّلْ مِنَّاۖ إِنَّكَ أَنتَ ٱلسَّمِيعُ ٱلْعَلِيمُ ١٢٧

And ´remember˥ when Ibrahim raised the foundation of the House with Ishmael, ´both praying,˥ "Our Lord! Accept ´this˥ from us. You are indeed the All-Hearing, All-Knowing.

Bukhari recorded that Ibn `Abbas said,

"Prophet Ibrahim took Ismail and his mother and went away with them until he reached the area of the House, where he left them next to a tree above Zamzam in the upper area of the Masjid. During that time, Ismail's mother was still nursing him. Makkah was then uninhabited, and there was no water source in it. Ibrahim left them there with a bag containing some dates and a water-skin containing water. Ibrahim then started to leave, and Ismail's mother followed him and said,

`O Ibrahim! To whom are you leaving us in this barren valley that is not inhabited'

She repeated the question several times and Ibrahim did not reply.

She asked, *'Has Allah commanded you to do this?'* He said, 'Yes.' She said, *"I am satisfied that Allah will never abandon us.'* Ibrahim left, and when he was far enough away where they could not see him, he faced the House, raised his hands and supplicated, *'(O our Lord! I have made some of my offspring to dwell in an uncultivable valley by Your Sacred House (the Kaaba at Makkah)'* (14:37).

Ismail's mother then returned to her place, started drinking water from the water-skin and nursing Ismail. When the water was used up, she and her son became thirsty. She looked at him, and he was suffering from thirst; she left to find water.

She found the nearest mountain, As-Safa, ascended it and looked, in vain. When she came down to the valley, she raised her garment and ran, just as a tired person runs, until she reached the Al-Marwah mountain. In vain, she looked to see if there was someone there. She ran to and fro (between the two mountains) seven times."

"When she reached Al-Marwah, she found the angel digging with his heel (or his wing) where Zamzam now exists, and the water gushed out. Ismail's mother was astonished and started digging, using her hand to transfer water to the water-skin."

"Ismail's mother started drinking the water and her milk increased for her child.

Afterwards some people of the tribe of Jurhum settled there. Time went on and Ismail grew into a righteous and learned young man.

Later on, her boy reached the age of puberty and married a lady from them, for Ismail learned Arabic from them, and they liked the way he was raised. Ismail's mother died after that.

Then an idea occurred to Ibrahim to visit his dependents. So he left (to Makkah). When he arrived, he did not find Ismail, so he asked his wife about him. She said, "He has gone out hunting.' When he asked her about their living conditions, she complained to him that they live in misery and poverty. Ibrahim said (to her), 'When your husband comes, convey my greeting and tell him to change the threshold of his gate.' When Ismail came, he sensed that they had a visitor and asked his wife, "Did we have a visitor?" She said, "Yes. An old man came to visit us and asked me about you, and I told him where you were. He also asked about our condition, and I told him that we live in hardship and poverty.' Ismail said, 'Did he ask you to do anything?' She said, "Yes. He asked me to convey his greeting and that you should change the threshold of your gate.' Ismail said to her, 'He was my father and you are the threshold, so go to your family (i.e. you are divorced).' So he divorced her and married another woman. Again

Ibrahim thought of visiting his dependents whom he had left (at Makkah). Ibrahim came to Ismail's house, but did not find Ismail and asked his wife, "Where is Ismail?" Ismail's wife replied, `He has gone out hunting.' He asked her about their condition, and she said that they have a good life and praised Allah. Ibrahim asked, "What is your food and what is your drink?' She replied, `Our food is meat and our drink is water.' He said, `O Allah! Bless their meat and their drink.'"

"Ibrahim said, 'When Ismail comes back, convey my greeting to him and ask him to keep the threshold of his gate.' When Ismail came back, he asked, 'Has anyone visited us?' She said, "Yes. A good looking old man,' and she praised Ibrahim, 'And he asked me about our livelihood and I told him that we live in good conditions.' He asked, `Did he ask you to convey any message?' She said, "Yes. He conveyed his greeting to you and said that you should keep the threshold of your gate.' Ismail said, 'That was my father, and you are the threshold; he commanded me to keep you.'

Ibrahim then came back visiting and found Ismail behind the Zamzam well, next to a tree, mending his arrows. When he saw Ibrahim, he stood up and they greeted each other. Ibrahim said, 'O Ismail, Your Lord has ordered me to do something.' He said, "Obey your Lord.' He asked Ismail, "Will you help me?" He said, "Yes, I will help you.' Ibrahim said, `Allah has commanded me to build a house for Him there, ' and he pointed to an area that was above ground level.

Ibrahim and Ismail searched for a suitable site to build the Kaaba. They found a site that had been marked with the footprint of the angel Jibril and the Prophet Ibrahim recognized it as the location he was shown in his dream.

Ibrahim and Ismail then began the construction of the Kaaba. They dug the foundation and laid the stones while reciting prayers and supplications to Allah.

The Prophet Ibrahim put the Black Stone, which was sent down from heaven, into its place in one of the corners of the Kaaba.

When the walls of the Kaaba were completed, Ibrahim stood on a rock and called out to the people of Mecca to come and perform the Hajj pilgrimage to the Kaaba.

The story of their construction of the Kaaba is a symbol of faith, sacrifice, and devotion to Allah.

Story Number 28:

Allah raised Isa a.s to the Heavens

Surah al-Nisa 157-159

وَقَوْلِهِمْ إِنَّا قَتَلْنَا ٱلْمَسِيحَ عِيسَى ٱبْنَ مَرْيَمَ رَسُولَ ٱللَّهِ وَمَا قَتَلُوهُ وَمَا صَلَبُوهُ وَلَٰكِن شُبِّهَ لَهُمْ ۚ وَإِنَّ ٱلَّذِينَ ٱخْتَلَفُوا۟ فِيهِ لَفِى شَكٍّ مِّنْهُ ۚ مَا لَهُم بِهِۦ مِنْ عِلْمٍ إِلَّا ٱتِّبَاعَ ٱلظَّنِّ ۚ وَمَا قَتَلُوهُ يَقِينًۢا ١٥٧

And for boasting, "We killed the Messiah, Isa A.S., son of Mary, the messenger of Allah." But they neither killed nor crucified him—it was only made to appear so. Even those who argue for this ˹crucifixion˺ are in doubt. They have no knowledge whatsoever—only making assumptions. They certainly did not kill him.

بَل رَّفَعَهُ ٱللَّهُ إِلَيْهِ ۚ وَكَانَ ٱللَّهُ عَزِيزًا حَكِيمًا ١٥٨

Rather, Allah raised him up to Himself. And Allah is Almighty, All-Wise.

In the materialistic age of luxury and worship of gold, Isa A.S. called his people to a nobler life by word and deed.

Isa A.S. called people to denounce worship of stone and gold, and the jewish pharisees (*Parsi*), and return to the law of Musa A.S.

Isa A.S. continued inviting the people to Almighty Allah. However, Isa A.S. was in conflict with the Jews' superficial interpretation of the Torah. He said that he did not come to abrogate the Torah, but to complete it.

His teaching annoyed the priests, for every word of Isa A.S. was a threat to them and their position, exposing their misdeeds.

The Roman occupiers had, at first, no intention of being involved in this religious discord of the Jews because it was an internal affair.

Isa A.S. continued his mission, aided by divine miracles. Some Quranic commentators said that Isa A.S. brought four people back from the dead. These had died during his lifetime. When the Jews saw this they said: "You only resurrect those who have died recently; perhaps they only fainted." They asked him to bring back to life Sam the Ibn Noah.

When he asked them to show him his grave, the people accompanied him there. Isa A.S. invoked Allah the Exalted to bring him back to life and behold, Sam the Ibn Noah came out from the grave gray-haired. Isa A.S. asked: *"how did you get gray hair, when there was no aging in your time?"* He answered: *"O Isa! I thought that the Day of Resurrection had come; from the fear of that day my hair turned gray."*

The forces of evil accused him of magic, infringement of the Mosaic Law, association with the devil; and when they saw that the poor people followed him, they began to scheme against him.

The Sanhedrin, the highest judicial council of the Jews, began to meet to plot against Isa A.S. When the Jews failed to stop Isa A.S.'s call, they decided to kill him. The chief priests held secret meetings to agree on the best way of getting rid of Isa A.S..

While they were in such a meeting, one of the twelve apostles of Isa A.S., Judas Iscariot, went to them and asked: "What will you give me if I deliver him to you?" Judas bargained with them until they agreed to give him thirty pieces of silver known as shekels. The plot was laid for the capture and murder of Isa A.S.

What happened was that Allah saved him from his enemies and raised him to heaven. They never killed Isa A.S.; they killed someone else.

Almighty Allah also revealed: And (remember) when Allah said: *"0 Isa A.S.! I will take you and raise you to Myself and clear you (of the forged statement that Isa A.S. is Allah son) of those who disbelieve, and I will make those who follow you (Monotheists, who worship none but Allah) superior to those who disbelieve (in the Oneness of Allah, or disbelieve in some of His Messengers, e.g. Muhammad, Isa A.S., Musa A.S., etc., or in His Holy Books, e.g. the Torah, the Gospel, the Qur'an) till the Day of Resurrection. Then you will return to Me and I will judge between you in the matters in which you used to dispute.* Quran Ayah 3:55

Story Number 29:

Quran condemns Abu-Lahab

Surah al-Lahab 1-5

تَبَّتْ يَدَآ أَبِى لَهَبٍ وَتَبَّ ١

May the hands of Abu Lahab perish, and he ˹himself˺ perish!

مَآ أَغْنَىٰ عَنْهُ مَالُهُ وَمَا كَسَبَ ٢

Neither his wealth nor ˹worldly˺ gains will benefit him.

سَيَصْلَىٰ نَارًا ذَاتَ لَهَبٍ ٣ وَٱمْرَأَتُهُ حَمَّالَةَ ٱلْحَطَبِ ٤ فِى جِيدِهَا حَبْلٌ مِّن مَّسَدٍ ٥

He will burn in a flaming Fire, and ˹so will˺ his wife, the carrier of ˹thorny˺ kindling, around her neck will be a rope of palm-fiber.

In the Qur'an, there is only one place where a person who was an enemy of Islam is named and condemned. This person is Abu Lahab, who was just as hostile to Islam and Prophet Muhammad as other people in Mecca and Medina. However, Abu Lahab is the only person who was mentioned in the Quran by name. So, what was so special about this person?

In ancient Arabia, there was chaos, bloodshed, and plunder. A person's life, honor, and property were only

protected if they had the support of their family and rela-
tives. Therefore, a strong bond between family members
was highly valued, and breaking this bond was a great
sin. When the Prophet began to preach Islam, the Bani
Hashim and Bani Al-Muttalib supported him openly, even
though they had not yet believed in his Prophethood. This
support was according to the moral traditions of Arabia,
and the other clans did not object to it. However, Abu
Lahab broke this moral principle because of his hostility
towards Islam. Abu Lahab was an uncle of the Prophet, and
in Arabia, an uncle was expected to look after his nephew
as his own child, especially if the nephew was fatherless.
But Abu Lahab refused to look after the Prophet, opposed
him publicly, and even asked his sons to divorce their
wives, who were the Prophet's daughters.

During the 7th year of Prophethood, all of the clans
of Quraysh boycotted Bani Hashim and Bani Al-Muttalib,
who were besieged in Shi'b Abi Talib. Abu Lahab was the
only person who sided with the disbelieving Quraysh
against his own clan. The boycott continued for three
years, and the Bani Hashim and Bani Al-Muttalib began
to starve. When a trade caravan came to Makkah, Abu
Lahab would shout out to the merchants to demand a forbidding price, so the poor customer would return empty-
handed to his starving children. Then, Abu Lahab would
purchase the same articles from them at the market rate.
This man was condemned in the Surah by name because
it was against the established traditions of Arabia for

an uncle to oppose his nephew without a reason or pelt stones and bring false accusations against him publicly.

His wife, Arwa bint Harb, nicknamed Umm Jameel, was the sister of the then enemy of Islam, Abu Sufyan. Although a real aunt, she used to throw thorny bushes in the path of the Prophet (SAW). The Holy Quran chastised both Abu Lahab and his wife in Surah Lahab and both of them died a miserable death as disbelievers.

Story Number 30:

When Ibrahim was in Fire

Surah Al-Anbiya 67-69

أُفٍّ لَّكُمْ وَلِمَا تَعْبُدُونَ مِن دُونِ ٱللَّهِ ۖ أَفَلَا تَعْقِلُونَ ٦٧

Shame on you and whatever you worship instead of Allah! Do you not have any sense?"

قَالُواْ حَرِّقُوهُ وَٱنصُرُوٓاْ ءَالِهَتَكُمْ إِن كُنتُمْ فَاعِلِينَ ٦٨

They concluded, "Burn him up to avenge your gods, if you must act."

قُلْنَا يَٰنَارُ كُونِى بَرْدًا وَسَلَٰمًا عَلَىٰٓ إِبْرَٰهِيمَ ٦٩

We ordered, "O fire! Be cool and safe for Ibrahim!"

In the kingdom of Babylon, idols were worshiped as though they were gods. Ibrahim's father Aazer was a well-known sculptor and he would craft idols from stone or wood. As a child, Ibrahim would watch his father work, often using the finished idols as playthings.

Ibrahim couldn't understand why people were worshiping these ornaments of stone in the temples. His father explained that the statues represented gods and people would offer them food and other gifts whilst asking for favors. This explanation didn't satisfy Ibrahim. In his heart, he felt that it was wrong.

As he grew older, Ibrahim became even more convinced that the idols his people worshiped were false. He would often question, 'how could statues of wood and stone be gods?' Especially considering the statues would have no power to either benefit or harm, being mere objects.

One night, Ibrahim traveled up to a mountain to watch the sky and observe nature. A while later, Ibrahim heard a voice calling him – it was none other than his Lord, Allah. He commanded Ibrahim to submit and become a Muslim.

Trembling, Ibrahim fell to the ground. He prostrated himself before Allah, crying out: "I submit to the Lord of the universe!" Eventually, he got to his feet and made his way back home. Ibrahim's life was forever transformed – and his heart was filled with great peace.

Ibrahim now had a mission – to call his people to the Truth and help them accept Allah as their one true God. First, he turned to his father who he loved so dearly. Ibrahim said: "O Father! Why do you worship that which doesn't hear, doesn't see, and cannot avail you in anything? O father, I have got knowledge which you have not, so follow me. I will guide you to a straight path." [Quran 19:42-48] Angrily, his father rejected Ibrahim's request and told his son to get out of his sight.

Undeterred, Ibrahim decided to channel his efforts towards bringing the people of his town towards the message of Allah, but they rejected his words and threatened him with violence. Ibrahim was given inspiration to adopt a different approach to change the hearts and minds of his people.

On the eve of a big celebration, Ibrahim knew that the townsfolk would be leaving to share a huge feast. When they had left, Ibrahim went into their temple to carry out a prophet mission: to demolish their idols, except one, the largest idol, so that he could explain to them the error of their ways.

When the townspeople returned, they were horrified. Their idols lay in ruins. They quickly remembered that Ibrahim had been encouraging them to worship Allah alone and to submit to the monotheistic faith of Ibrahim. They asked him: "are you the one who has done this?" Ibrahim said no. "This statue, the biggest of them all, has done it! Ask them about it!" The townspeople replied: "You know they cannot speak!" And Ibrahim said: "Then how can you worship things that can neither speak or see. They can't even protect themselves. Have you all lost your minds?"

They were silent, knowing that Ibrahim had made a valid point, but their pride wouldn't allow them to reject the idols they'd been worshiping for generations. Anger surged in the crowd.

The crowd bayed for Ibrahim to be burned. They wanted revenge for the damage to their idols and only Ibrahim's blood would do. The decision to burn him alive was sanctioned by Nimrod, the king of Babylon, and his priests. News traveled fast and thousands of people from all over the kingdom arrived to witness the execution.

A huge pit was dug in the ground and filled with wood. It was the biggest fire anyone had ever seen. Ibrahim was shackled, his hands and feet chained tightly together, and he was fitted into a giant catapult that would throw him in the fire.

At that moment, Ibrahim was visited by the Angel Jibreel, who said: "Is there anything you wish for?". Ibrahim replied that his only wish was for Allah to be pleased with him. He could've asked for anything, but instead of begging for his life to be saved, he chose to ask for the blessing of God.

Allah would not allow the Prophet to be executed. He ordered the fire to be nothing but cool and peaceful for Ibrahim, and the fire obeyed, burning only Ibrahim's chains. Ibrahim walked out the fire without a bead of sweat upon his skin or hint of smoke coming from his clothing. Spectators gasped in amazement, crying: "*Ibrahim's God has saved him from the flames!*"

Conclusion

'Learn the Quran in 30 Days of Ramadan' has been a humble effort to offer a unique perspective on the holy book of Islam. Through the lens of thirty carefully selected stories, it takes you on a journey of spiritual growth and development, learning important lessons about faith, morality, and the divine nature of the Quran.

Each story is presented with clarity and depth, providing us with a clear understanding of the themes and messages conveyed in the Quran. Whether you are a devout Muslim seeking to deepen your understanding of the holy Quran, or a curious reader interested in exploring the teachings of Islam, this book offers something valuable for everyone.

Above all, *'Learn the Quran in 30 Days of Ramadan'* reminds us that the Quran is a source of wisdom, guidance, and inspiration that can help us navigate life's challenges with grace and dignity. By studying its teachings and reflecting on its stories, we can cultivate a deeper connection with our faith and develop a stronger sense of purpose and meaning in our lives.

I hope that this book serves as a valuable resource for readers seeking to deepen their understanding of the Quran and I pray that it inspires all those who read it to continue on their journey of spiritual growth and development.

Duas to Heighten your Imaan

Muhammad SAW said:

'Faith wears out in your hearts the way that your garments would wear out' (Mustadrak al-Haakim).

It is natural for the imaan, our faith to weaken, or sometimes fade away, just like a garment does even if it is taken care of. While we pray five times a day, and fast in the month of Ramdan, and recite the Quran, it is still important to ask Allah to strengthen our faith, to revive our Iman.

Here are some hadith and duas that guide us on how to revive our faith.

Mu'adh R.A. reported:

The Messenger of Allah SAW took hold of my hand and said:

"O Mu'adh! By Allah I love you, so I advise you to never forget to recite after every prayer:

اللهم أعني على ذكرك وشكرك، وحسن عبادتك.

'O Allah, help me remember You, to be grateful to You, and to worship You in an excellent manner.'

[Abu Dawud]

Shahr bin Hawshab said:

"I said to Umm Salamah: 'O Mother of the Believers! What was the supplication that the Messenger of Allah SAW said most frequently when he was with you?"

She said: 'The supplication he said most frequently was:

يَا مُقَلِّبَ الْقُلُوبِ ثَبِّتْ قَلْبِي عَلَى دِينِكَ

"Oh turner of the hearts (Allah, the Most High), keep our hearts firm on your religion" (Al-Tirmadhi)

Ali R.A. reported: The Messenger of Allah SAW said to me, *'Recite:*

اللَّهُمَّ اهْدِنِى ، وسَدِّدْنِى

O Allah! Guide me and grant me success'

Dua

Bismillahir Rahmanir Rahim

اللَّهُمَّ صَلِّ عَلَى مُحَمَّدٍ وَعَلَى آلِ مُحَمَّدٍ كَمَا صَلَّيْتَ عَلَى إِبْرَاهِيمَ وَعَلَى آلِ إِبْرَاهِيمَ، ،إِنَّكَ حَمِيدٌ مَجِيدٌ

اللَّهُمَّ بَارِكْ عَلَى مُحَمَّدٍ وَعَلَى آلِ مُحَمَّدٍ كَمَا بَارَكْتَ عَلَى إِبْرَاهِيمَ وَعَلَى آلِ إِبْرَاهِيمَ، إِنَّكَ حَمِيدٌ مَجِيدٌ

O the Mighty one! The Merciful! O Creator! O *La Shareek!*

We have come to you for our petty desires.

You are disappointed with us. Our *Aa'mal* have disappointed you. We got absorbed by the affairs of this mortal life so much that we forgot about the afterlife.

Oh Allah, we turn to You in humility and gratitude. We seek Your infinite mercy, forgiveness, and blessings. We recognize that You are the Most Merciful, the Most Gracious, and the Most Compassionate, and we beseech Your divine favor upon us.

Oh Allah, we pray that You accept all our good deeds and forgive our sins.

We ask for Your mercy and blessings upon our families, our friends, and all the believers around the world.

We pray for those who are suffering, those who are oppressed, and those who are in need. We ask that You alleviate their pain, grant them relief, and guide them towards the path of righteousness.

Oh Allah, we ask that You bless us with good health, happiness, and prosperity. We pray for Your protection and guidance in all aspects of our lives. We ask that You grant us the strength to overcome any challenges that we may face, and to always remain steadfast in our faith.

Oh Allah, on this special night of Qadr, we ask that You grant us Your divine blessings and mercy. We pray that You accept our *duas* and grant us our most cherished desires. We ask that You forgive our sins, and grant us the reward of the highest level of Jannah.

Oh Allah, we ask that You accept our fasting, our prayers, our charity, and all our good deeds during this blessed month of Ramzan.

We ask that You grant us the opportunity to witness many more Ramzan in our lives, and that You continue to bless us with Your infinite mercy and love.

Oh Allah, we thank You for all the blessings You have bestowed upon us, and we ask that You continue to shower us with Your mercy and blessings. Ameen.

Ya Rabbul Alameen.

Made in the USA
Las Vegas, NV
05 April 2023

70194023R00075